Collins

Cambridge Lower Secondary

English as a Second Language

Nick Coates

STAGE 7: STUDENT'S BOOK

HarperCollins 200 PUBLISHERS
Since 1817

William Collins' dream of knowledge for all began with the publication of his first book in 1819.

A self-educated mill worker, he not only enriched millions of lives, but also founded a flourishing publishing house. Today, staying true to this spirit, Collins books are packed with inspiration, innovation and practical expertise. They place you at the centre of a world of possibility and give you exactly what you need to explore it.

Collins. Freedom to teach.

Published by Collins
An imprint of HarperCollins*Publishers*
The News Building
1 London Bridge Street
London
SE1 9GF

Browse the complete Collins catalogue at
www.collins.co.uk

© HarperCollins*Publishers* Limited 2017

10 9 8 7 6 5 4 3 2 1

ISBN 978-0-00-821540-8

All rights reserved. No part of this publication may be reproduced, stored in a retrieval system, or transmitted in any form by any means, electronic, mechanical, photocopying, recording or otherwise, without the prior written permission of the Publisher or a licence permitting restricted copying in the United Kingdom issues by the Copyright Licensing Agency Ltd., Barnard's Inn, 86 Fetter Lane, London, EC4A 1EN.

British Library Cataloguing in Publication Data
A catalogue record for this publication is available from the British Library.

Author: Nick Coates
Development editor: Helen King
Series editor: Nick Coates
Commissioning editor: Lucy Cooper
In-house editor: Caroline Green/Lara McMurray
Project manager: Anna Stevenson
Copyeditor: Donatella Montrone
Answer checker: Sonya Newland
Proofreader: Karen Williams
Illustrator: QBS Learning/Jouve India Private Ltd/Nick Coates
Photo researcher: Sophie Hartley
Cover designer: Kevin Robbins
Cover illustrator: Maria Herbert-Liew
Typesetter: Jouve India Private Ltd
Audio: ID Audio
Production controller: Rachel Weaver
Printed and bound by: Grafica Veneta in Italy

MIX
Paper from responsible sources
www.fsc.org FSC™ C007454

This book is produced from independently certified FSC paper to ensure responsible forest management.

For more information visit:
www.harpercollins.co.uk/green

Contents

Contents map		4
Unit 1	Language and communication	7
Unit 2	Shops and shopping	17
Review 1		27
Unit 3	Catching the criminals	29
Unit 4	Dragons	39
Review 2		49
Unit 5	Art	51
Unit 6	Adventure sports	61
Review 3		71
Unit 7	The future of transport	73
Unit 8	Stories	83
Mid-year review		93
Unit 9	Wildlife under threat	99
Unit 10	Climate change	109
Review 4		119
Unit 11	Healthy living	121
Unit 12	Game shows	131
Review 5		141
Unit 13	Rivers and bridges	143
Unit 14	Hobbies	153
Review 6		163
Unit 15	Space travel	165
Unit 16	Science fiction	175
End-of-year review		185
Key word list		191

Contents map

Unit / Topic	Reading	Listening	Speaking	Writing	Use of English
1 Language and communication	• World languages (informational text) • Using reference resources	• Communicating without words	• Greetings • Discussion: language learning	• Dialogue: language learning	• Indefinite pronouns • Present perfect tense (for recent events)
Project: sign language					
Focus on ICT: social media					
2 Shops and shopping	• Where do you shop? (short descriptive texts)	• Shopping conversations	• Role play: shopping	• Punctuation of direct speech • Dialogue: shopping	• Quantifiers • Comparing (not as + adjective + as) • Modals: have to
Project: shopping experiences					
Focus on the World: three of the best markets					
Review 1					
3 Catching the criminals	• Newspaper reports of crimes	• A police report	• Discussion: ranking crimes • Reporting a crime	• A police report • Spelling and punctuation	• Passive forms (past simple) • Reported speech
Project: a blurb for a crime story					
Focus on Science: forensic science					
4 Dragons	• Komodo dragons (a web page)	• A story	• Discussion: dragons • Presenting animal facts • Retelling a story	• A webpage about an animal	• Present perfect tense (for unfinished events) • Modals: can • Reported speech (said and told)
Project: a festival					
Focus on Literature: a folk tale					
Review 2					
5 Art	• Newspaper article on modern art	• A description of a painting	• Discussions: statements about art and making art from rubbish	• Describing a painting (making a response and giving an opinion)	• Relative clauses (non-defining) • Abstract nouns • Similes with like and as
Project: a work of art					
Focus on Art: art of ancient Africa					
6 Adventure sports	• Three adventure sports (informational text)	• Interview with the manager of an activities company	• Describing an adventure sport	• A description of an adventure sport	• Compound nouns and adjectives • Conjunctions of time • Prepositions + ing

Unit / Topic	Reading	Listening	Speaking	Writing	Use of English
Project: a timetable (for an adventure weekend)					
Focus on the World: national sports					
Review 3					
7 The future of transport	• Green cars (infographic)	• A news report	• Brainstorming and categorising forms of transport • Discussion: the future of transport	• An infographic on Maglev trains	• Conjunctions *as* and *since* • Future forms (*will* and *(be) going to*)
Project: the future of transport					
Focus on Geography: urbanisation and traffic management					
8 Stories	• What makes a good story? (informational text)	• A folk tale	• Summarising a story • Telling a story	• Planning and starting a story	• Reported speech (questions) • Participles used as adjectives
Project: *The map* (planning and writing a story)					
Focus on Literature: three poems					
Mid-year review					
9 Wildlife under threat	• Good news for one endangered cat (magazine article)	• A talk by a scientist about endangered animals	• Role play: a meeting	• A report of a meeting	• Modals • Noun phrases • Conjunctions *so … that* and *such … that* • *why* clauses
Project: endangered animals					
Focus on Biology: classification					
10 Climate change	• So what if Earth gets a tiny bit warmer? (informational text)	• A woman talks about the impact of climate change on her life	• Discussion: ways to save energy	• A magazine article	• Intensifying adverbs • Unlikely (second) conditional • Multi-word verbs
Project: reducing climate change					
Focus on the World: winds of the world					
Review 4					
11 Healthy living	• Attitudes to diet and exercise • Top tips … for healthy living (blog post)	• A lecture by a health specialist on dieting	• Discussion: experiences of diets	• Attitude to diet and exercise • A lifestyle diary	• Present perfect tense (for experience) • Sentence adverbs • Gerund as subject and object
Project: a healthy lifestyles questionnaire					
Focus on Health Science: nutrient food groups					

Unit / Topic	Reading	Listening	Speaking	Writing	Use of English
12 Game shows	• The world's favourite game show (webpage)	• A quiz	• Discussion: wishes • Play a quiz game	• Questions for a quiz	• Prepositional phrases • *wish* clauses • Question forms
Project: *Who Wants to be a Millionaire?*					
Focus on Literature: *Q&A*					
Review 5					
13 Rivers and bridges	• Account of a river journey (three blog posts)	• Three people describing bridges	• Discussion: plans	• A blog post (about a journey)	• Past continuous tense • Past perfect tense
Project: a river adventure (planning a journey)					
Focus on History: Ancient Egypt					
14 Hobbies	• Three of the strangest hobbies (web page)	• Instructions to make something	• Discussion: hobbies • Give a talk about a hobby	• Introducing a hobby	• Relative clauses (defining) • Gerund and infinitive forms after verbs
Project: a new hobby					
Focus on the World: hobbies around the world					
Review 6					
15 Space travel	• The International Space Station (informational text)	• A talk about the history of space travel	• A balloon debate: jobs	• A formal report giving reasons and explanations	• Position of adverbs in sentences • Adjective + dependent preposition • Multi-word verbs • Passive forms (present simple)
Project: life on the ISS					
Focus on Maths: calculating our weight on other planets					
16 Science fiction	• Science fiction predictions that became fact (informational text)	• A science fiction story	• Discussion: what is science fiction? • Making predictions	• Planning a story	• Pre-determiners (quantifying) • Causative forms • Future forms (present simple and continuous)
Project: a science fiction story					
Focus on Literature: *Eager*					
End-of year review					

Language and communication

1

Looking forward

This unit explores different ways in which we use language, why we learn languages, as well as various types of communication.

You will read
- about different languages around the world
- about social media
- about sign languages

You will listen
- to people expressing feelings using sounds and tone of voice

You will speak
- about greetings and who to use them with
- about learning languages

You will write
- a conversation with a foreign student

You will learn
- about indefinite pronouns (*nobody*, *anything*, *everyone*, and so on)
- to talk about recent events using the present perfect tense

Using language

Speaking: greetings

Work in groups. Read the questions and discuss.

- Who do you greet first in the morning? What do you say?
- Do you greet everyone you meet in the same way? What do you say to different people?
- Do you greet anyone in a different language? What do you say?
- How many languages can you greet people in?

Speaking: language learning

Work in groups. Discuss.

- Read what these language students say. Who do you agree with?

Anika says, "I love learning languages. It's fun! It means I can talk to someone in another country. We should all learn as many languages as possible at school."

Paulo says, "I think everybody should learn and use the same language. Then we can all communicate easily."

Femi says, "My home language is the most important language. We should use it all the time at school and not use English."

Lin says, "English is used all over the world so it's good to learn it. But I would like to keep learning and using my home language too."

formal and informal register; give an opinion

Writing: a conversation

1 Read the fact files to find out more about the four language students.
- Which one would you like to meet and talk to?
- What would you talk about?
- Do you agree with what he / she says about language learning?

Name:	Anika
Nationality:	German
Home language:	German
Other languages:	English, French, Russian
Hobbies:	tennis, reading

Name:	Paulo
Nationality:	Brazilian
Home language:	Portuguese
Other languages:	English, Spanish
Hobbies:	football, computer games

Name:	Femi
Nationality:	South African
Home language:	Zulu
Other languages:	English
Hobbies:	running, music

Name:	Lin
Nationality:	South Korean
Home language:	Korean
Other languages:	English, Chinese
Hobbies:	basketball, films

2 Imagine you meet one of the students. Write your conversation.
- Greet each other and introduce yourselves.

    Anika: Hi! My name's Anika. What is your name?

    [You]: Hello. I'm …

- Ask and answer questions to get to know each other.

    [You]: So, you love running. Me too! How far do you run?

    Femi: Not far. I run 100 and 200 metres. I like to run fast.

- Give your opinion about language learning.

    Paulo: I think everybody should learn and use the same language.

    [You]: I agree that's a good idea, but which language? In my opinion, we should all learn English, but I don't think everyone will agree.

3 In pairs, take turns to read out your conversations.

> **My learning**
> We learn by doing and then by thinking about what we did.
>
> Think about how the conversation sounded when you read it out.
>
> Can you make it better?

write a dialogue; give opinions

World languages

Reading: setting the scene

What do you think are the answers to these questions?
- How many languages are there in the world?
- Which language has the most speakers?
- Which language is the most important?

Reading: exploring the text

1 **Read the text. Check your answers to the questions above.**

> **How many languages are there in the world?**
>
> Nobody knows for sure. Most books say between 4000 and 5000, but some people say there are 10 000. We do know there are about 1000 languages spoken in Africa.
>
> **Which language has the most speakers?**
>
> Again, there is no simple answer to this question. The language with the most mother-tongue speakers is certainly Chinese. In China, around a billion people speak it. Not many people outside China can speak Chinese, but recently some people have started to learn it.
>
> Some countries have many different mother tongues, so people use one language to communicate with one another. This language might be used in other countries, too. It is called a 'world language' when it is spoken by many people in many countries. English, for example, is a world language used in 115 countries around the world. Spanish is another world language used in 20 countries. Some of these countries are very big, for example, South America, and there may be more speakers of Spanish than there are speakers of English.
>
> **Which language is the most important?**
>
> Another difficult question! Everyone will say that their own language is the most important. However, world languages are important because they can be used in so many countries. Languages used at the United Nations are Chinese, English, French, Russian, Spanish and Arabic. English is used in some jobs around the world, for example, by pilots or oil workers.

2 **Look at how the text is written.**
  1 How many sections are there in the text?
  2 What starts each section?
  3 What is the rest of each section?

read for specific information

Reading: look it up

1 If you find a word or information in a text you don't understand, which of these do you do?
- a keep reading because you don't have to understand every word
- b ask a friend or parent for help
- c ask a teacher for help
- d look it up in a book
- e look it up online

2 Match the types of information to where you can look it up.

I need to …
1 find out about continents and countries
2 find out about other facts and information
3 find out about words

I can look it up in …
a an encyclopaedia
b a dictionary
c a map or an atlas

3 Look up the answers to these questions. Use a dictionary, an encyclopaedia or a map, either as books or online.
1 What does the word *continent* mean?
2 How many countries are there in Africa?
3 How many people live in China?

Vocabulary: words in context

1 Copy and complete the sentences using words from the text.
1 The language we learn first is our m_____ t_____ .
2 One b_____ is a thousand million (1 000 000 000).
3 In the past, only people in China spoke Chinese, but r_____ people in the rest of the world have started to learn it.
4 People all over the world need to c_____ with one another.

2 Find the names of two continents in the text on the previous page.
- Which continent do you live on?
- What other continents do you know?

3 How many languages are named in the text?

4 Can you speak any of the languages in the picture on page 7? Tell your class.

Did you know …?
You can find dictionaries, encyclopaedias and maps as books or online.

You can find a lot of help online, but ask an adult to help you find the best sites.

Did you know …?
There are seven continents in the world. Find them on a map.

There are no countries in the continent of Antarctica and no people live there.

Africa has the most countries.

Asia has the most people living there – about 4.5 billion people.

use reference resources 11

Use of English: *nobody, someone, everything*

1 Work in pairs. Look at what Anika and Paulo said about learning languages. Discuss these questions.

> … I can talk to <u>someone</u> in another country.
>
> I think <u>everybody</u> should learn and use the same language.

- Does *someone* tell us exactly who Anika can talk to?
- Does *everybody* tell us exactly which people should learn and use the language?
- Imagine that Anika and Paulo said:

> … I can talk to my friend Lin in South Korea.
>
> I think all the school children in the world should learn and use the same language.

What is the difference now?

2 Find two examples of these kinds of pronouns in the text on page 7.

3 Copy and complete the table with the correct pronouns.

everybody	everyone	everything
somebody	1	something
anybody	anyone	2
3	no one	nothing

Language tip
Someone and *everybody* are types of pronouns (words that stand in place of a noun, for example, *she, you, them*). We use them when we don't know, or don't want to say, exactly who or what we are talking about.

4 Copy and complete the sentences using pronouns from your completed table above.

1. I want to learn Arabic but I don't know _____ who can help me.

2. The box is empty. There's _____ here.

3. Quiet, children! I want _____ to listen to me.

4. I'm sorry you aren't well. Is there _____ I can do to help?

indefinite pronouns

Communicating without words

Listening: setting the scene

Read the text, then match the feelings to the pictures.

When we communicate with someone, we often use language – but not always. We can also communicate without language. Our faces can show what we are thinking or how we are feeling. People all around the world show six feelings with their faces. These show if they are happy, sad, surprised, angry, afraid or disgusted (when they don't like something).

happy   sad   surprised   angry   afraid   disgusted

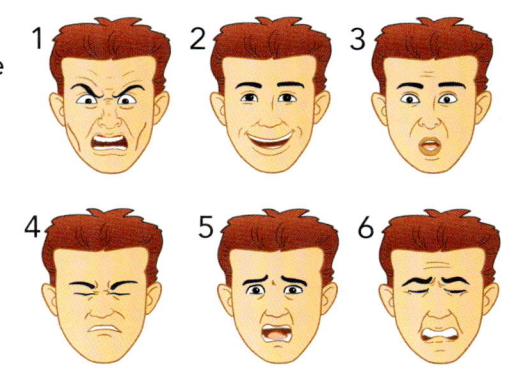

Listening: tone of voice

We can also show our feelings by the way we speak and the sounds we make.

1. 🔊 Listen to each person and match to one of the six feelings.

2. Listen again. Work in pairs to decide what has happened. Discuss:
   - who the person is, where they are and what they are doing
   - what happens to make the person feel angry, happy, and so on
   - what the people say before and after what you have heard.

3. Choose one of the situations you have discussed. Act it out for the class.

Use of English: present perfect tense

1. These sentences explain what has happened. Name the verb tense.
   - She's afraid because she <u>has seen</u> a snake.
   - He's angry because someone <u>has turned off</u> his computer.

2. Answer these questions to make the grammar rule for the verb tense.
   - Do we use this tense for something that *has happened recently* or for something that *happened a long time ago*?
   - Do we make this tense with *has / have* + past participle or with *was / were* + verb + *ing*?
   - When we talk about the recent past, can we use *just* or can we use *ago*? Where do we put it in the sentence?

3. Look in the reading text on page 10. Find an example of the present perfect which explains something that started recently.

tone of voice; present perfect tense   13

Focus on ICT

An introduction to social media for students

Many teenagers and young people have grown up with social media, but did you know that it only became really popular after 2000? It is now one of the most important forms of communication around the world, and it is still growing fast.

But what exactly is social media? It's the use of the internet from a computer or a **mobile device** so that people can communicate with one another. Social media differs from traditional media in that ordinary people can create and share information very quickly. Traditional media often needs a lot of professional people to take time to create information in a way that can be shared. For example, a newspaper can take a day to produce, a magazine can take a few weeks, a book can take many months and a film or TV series can take years. However, anyone can write a **tweet** in a few seconds!

Thousands of social media websites are available, but there are five general types that a lot of teenagers around the world use. The most popular type of social media are **social networking sites**. These allow people to stay in touch with their friends and to connect with other people of the same age or with similar interests. *Facebook* is the most successful social networking site, used by many people around the world. A second, similar type of social media is a **blog**, where users can communicate their thoughts, ideas, plans and so on, quickly to all their **followers**. The most popular of these is *Twitter*, which is called a **microblog** because all the messages (or tweets) must be very short. A third type of social media is a file-sharing site. Users can share videos, photos or **text** on these sites, and *YouTube* is the most well-known example. Then there are gaming sites, in which users **interact** with one another to play games, for example, *World of Warcraft*. A fifth type of social media is the project-type site. People who have similar interests can share their knowledge through a website. The biggest and most well-known of this type of site is *Wikipedia*, which contains a huge amount of useful information. Students can use this type of site for free to help with homework and projects – but must remember that the information is not always 100% accurate and that they cannot copy text from websites and use it as their own work.

Talking point

Social media is very important to our lives. Is it always a good thing? Can you think of any bad things about using social media?

read extended non-fiction text

1 Find these words in the text. Then match them with their meaning.

1. mobile device
2. tweet
3. social networking site
4. blog
5. microblog
6. followers
7. text
8. interact

a. a piece of writing
b. to talk or do things with other people
c. a small computer (for example, a smartphone, notebook or laptop) that you can carry around
d. a website containing thoughts, ideas or information that is often added to
e. people who ask for and receive blogs or tweets from someone else
f. a website where people communicate with friends
g. a blog of only a few words for each entry
h. a message put on Twitter

2 Read the first two paragraphs of the text.

1. When did social media begin?
   a. Before 2000
   b. In 2000
   c. After 2000
2. What is *social media*?
   a. What you do on a computer.
   b. A form of communication using the internet.
   c. When you talk to your friends or family.
3. Name four examples of traditional media.
4. Name two ways in which social media and traditional media are different.
5. Name one way in which social media and traditional media are the same.

3 Read the third paragraph of the text. Copy and complete the diagram.

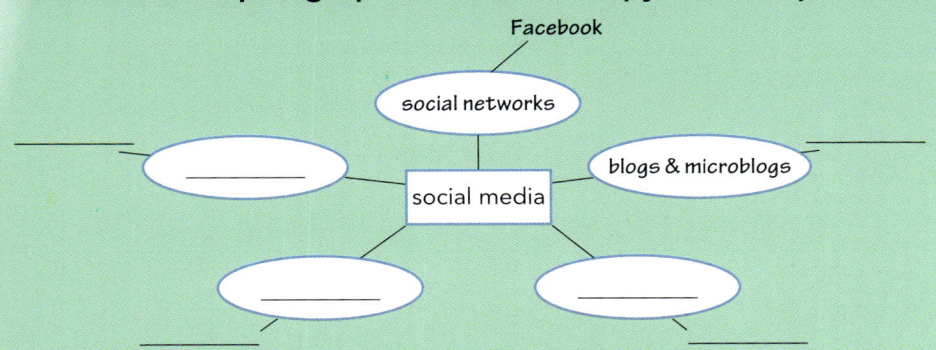

- social media
  - social networks
    - Facebook
  - blogs & microblogs
  - _____
  - _____
  - _____

4 Can you think of any other social media sites? Add them to your diagram, in the correct place.

5 Work in groups. Discuss the Talking point. In your notebook, write three good points and three bad points about using social media.

read extended non-fiction text 15

Project: sign language

In this first project, you are going to learn to communicate with each other using a sign language.

People who are not able to hear or speak use sign language. There are different signs, in the same way as there are different languages. There are about 300 sign languages used around the world, and each sign language uses different signs. In fact, people who use American Sign Language will not be able to understand someone who uses British Sign Language.

FRIEND

The sign for friend in American Sign Language

Finger spelling is another kind of sign language. Each letter of the alphabet has its own sign – see the table. You can learn the signs quickly and they can be used to spell out any word. However, this kind of sign language is slow to use.

1 Think of a short question to ask your partner. Use the table to work out the correct finger spelling for the question.

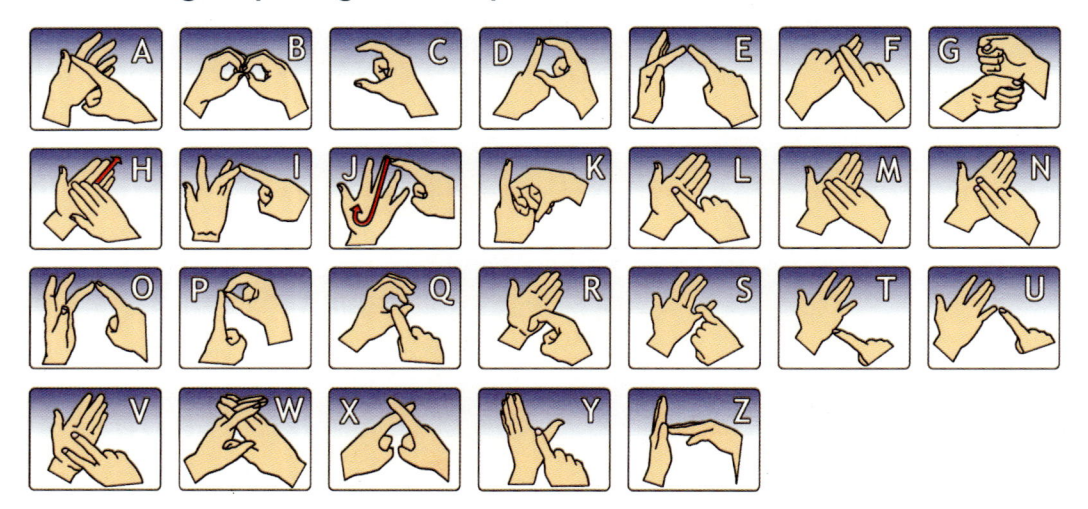

2 With your partner, take turns to ask and answer your question. Remember not to talk!

- Student A asks a question using finger spelling. Student B uses the table to understand the question.
- Student B answers the question using finger spelling. Student A uses the table to understand the answer.
- Change roles.

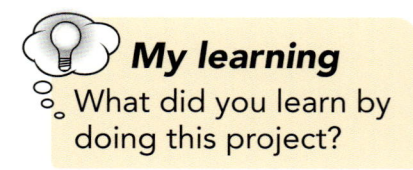

My learning
What did you learn by doing this project?

interact with peers to negotiate a task

Shops and shopping 2

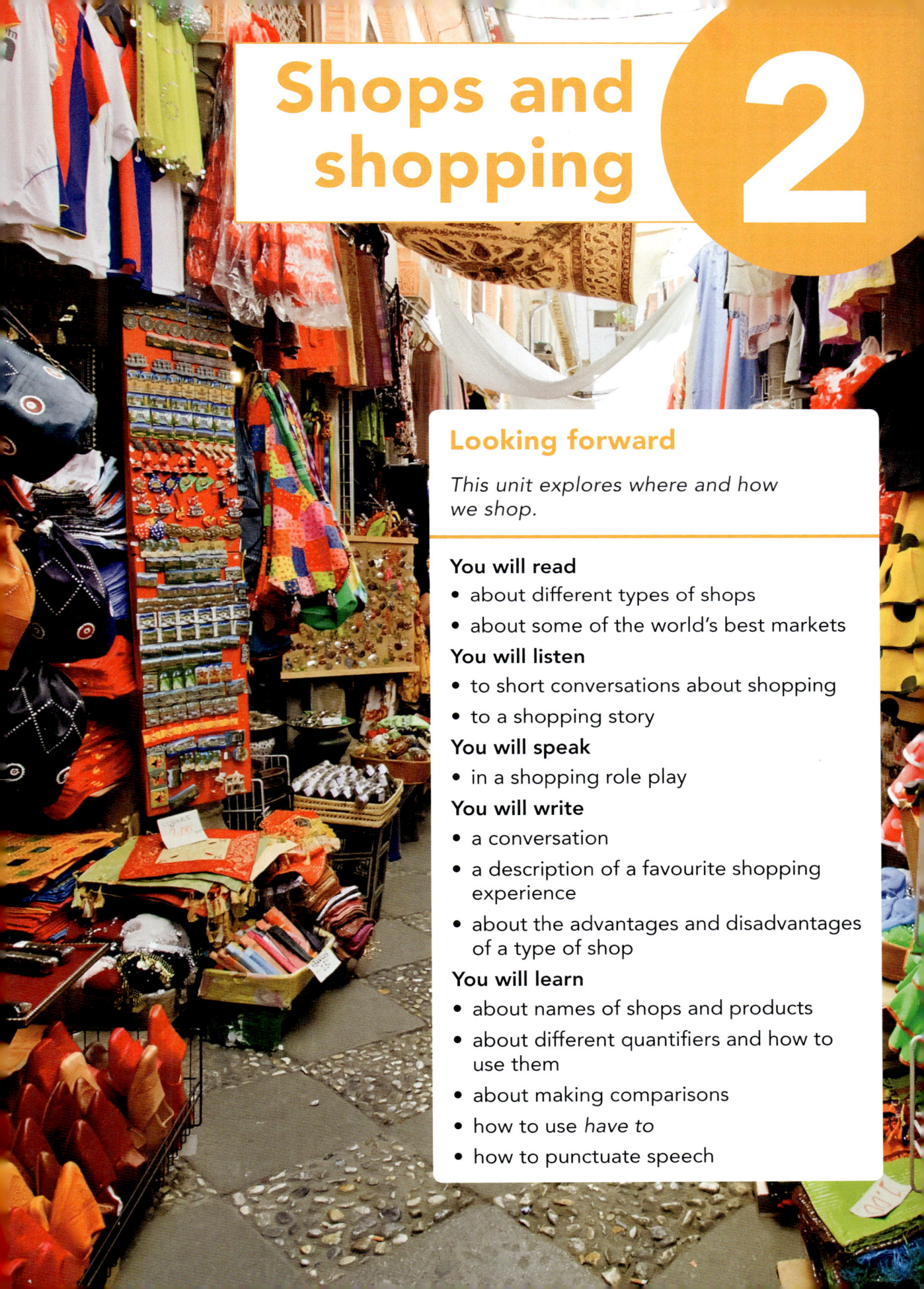

Looking forward

This unit explores where and how we shop.

You will read
- about different types of shops
- about some of the world's best markets

You will listen
- to short conversations about shopping
- to a shopping story

You will speak
- in a shopping role play

You will write
- a conversation
- a description of a favourite shopping experience
- about the advantages and disadvantages of a type of shop

You will learn
- about names of shops and products
- about different quantifiers and how to use them
- about making comparisons
- how to use *have to*
- how to punctuate speech

Where do you shop?

Reading: setting the scene

Discuss.
- Do you like shopping? Why / Why not?
- Where do you go shopping? Who do you like to go with?
- Do you know what these six types of shops are? What can you buy in each shop?

> department store   internet shopping   market
> mini-market   shopping mall   specialist shop

Reading: exploring the text

1 Read about different types of shops and match them to the photos a–f. Which type of shop does not have a photo?

Markets
People have shopped in markets since the earliest times. You can still find them all over the world and they are often the cheapest places to shop.

Supermarkets
These are like food markets under one roof. They are self-service – shoppers choose their own products and go to the checkout to pay for them.

Mini-markets
These are usually close to where people live, and can be very useful. They can have a good choice of products, for example, bread, rice, vegetables but are often more expensive than other shops.

Specialist shops
These sell just one type of product, for example, bread, cameras, books. You can find a large number of specialist stores in shopping malls – one store will sell clothes, one will sell shoes, one will sell jewellery, and so on.

Department stores
These are big stores that have many different parts, or departments. Each department is like a specialist shop. Department stores offer plenty of choice – *Harrods* in London says it has *All Things for All People, Everywhere*.

Shopping malls
For many people, these are the best shopping experience of all! They are in huge buildings. Inside there are lots of specialist shops, often a supermarket, and cafes, banks, cinemas, and so on.

Internet shopping
You can stay at home and shop using your computer, smartphone or TV. This type of shopping is convenient but not as interesting as visiting a market or a shopping mall.

2 Name an example of each type of shop near where you live.

discuss shopping; shop vocabulary

Reading: understanding the text

Read the text again and answer the questions.

1. Which is usually the cheapest?
2. Which can you do from home?
3. Which has shops and other places in the same building?
4. Which sells only one type of product?
5. Which is usually closest to your home?
6. Which do you prefer to use? Why?

Vocabulary: words in context

1. **Look at the text about *Supermarkets*. Find words that mean:**
   a when you help yourself to things in a shop or restaurant
   b the things you buy
   c the place where you pay.

2. **Look at the text about *Mini-markets*. Find a word (a noun) that means the things you can choose.**

3. **Look at the text about *Specialist shops*. Find a word (a noun) that means the same as a shop.**

4. **Look at the text about *Shopping malls*. Find words that mean:**
   a something that happens to you
   b very big.

5. **Look at the text about *Internet shopping*. Find a word that means near to where you are or where you want to go.**

Use of English: talking about quantity

1. **Look at the text about *Shopping malls*.**
   1. Does the word *many* tell us about the number of people, or does it tell us about the type of people?
   2. Does it tell us the exact number of people?
   3. Find a two-word phrase that means the same as *many*.

> *Language tip*
> Remember! **Countable nouns** are things we can count (for example, buildings, shops, products). We use *How many …?* to ask questions about them.
>
> **Uncountable nouns** are things we cannot count (for example, water, rice, bread), and they have no plurals. We use *How much …?* to ask questions about them.

read for specific information

2 Find two more phrases in the whole text that mean the same as *many*.

3 Which other words or phrases do you know that mean *many* or *not many*?

4 Play a game in a group. Talk about what you and your friends bought.
- Start: *I went shopping and I bought …*
- Choose a word or phrase in the box and the name of a product you bought.

> a large number of   a lot of / lots of   plenty of
> many   some   several   a few

- Listen to what your friends say. When it is your turn, say what they bought and then say what you bought.

Use of English: comparing

1 Look at the text about *Mini-markets*. Complete this sentence.

   Mini-markets are often … other shops.

2 Compare some people or things using these adjectives: *tall, cheap, interesting, good*.

   You're much taller than me!

3 When we want to compare people or things that have a big difference, we can use *much*. Compare some people or things using *much* and an adjective.

4 Read the text about *Internet shopping*. Complete this sentence.

   Internet shopping is … visiting a market or mall.

5 Change these sentences to use *not as … as …* Keep the same meaning and the same adjective.
1. Shopping in a supermarket is faster than shopping at a market.
2. I'm taller than you are.
3. Germany is colder than Egypt.
4. Visiting a mall is more interesting than going to a department store.

Language tip
When we compare with *not as … as …*, the first thing mentioned is always 'less' than the second.

quantifiers; comparing

Shopping stories

Listening: shopping conversations

1 🔊 **Listen to the first phone conversation. Where is Bella?**
   a   a shopping mall   b   a market   c   a supermarket

2 🔊 **Listen to the second phone conversation between Maria and her father. What's Maria doing?**
   a   shopping at the market
   b   shopping in a department store
   c   eating in a restaurant

3 🔊 **Listen to the third conversation. What did Adam want to buy?**
   a   brown shoes   b   grey shoes   c   black shoes

4 🔊 **Listen to the third conversation again. Order the pictures to tell Adam's story.**

   a   b   c   d

Use of English: *have to*

1 **In all of the conversations someone *had to do* something.**
   1   What did Bella have to do? Why?
   2   What did Maria have to do? Why?
   3   What did the man have to do twice? Why?

2 **Answer these questions about *have to*.**
   1   What is another word we can use instead of *have to*? I <u>have to</u> go to the shop now.
   2   What type and form of word always goes after *have to*?
   3   What is the past form of *have to*?
   4   What is the future form of *have to*?

3 **Work in pairs. Ask and answer.**

   What do you have to do every day?

   What did you have to do yesterday?

   What will you have to do next week?

listen for main points; listen to extended narrative; modal have to

Let's go shopping

Speaking: setting the scene

1. **You are going into a small specialist shop. Think about the conversation you will have.**
   - What do you say to the shop assistant?
   - What do you think the shop assistant will say to you?
   - How can you ask for something?
   - What else will you say?

2. **Look at the four specialist shops. Make a list of items sold in each shop.**
   - a newsagent
   - an electronics shop
   - a pharmacy
   - a jewellery shop

Speaking: role play

1. **Prepare for the shopping role play.**
   - Some of you will work in the shops. Read the list of what you have in your shop.
   - Some of you will be shoppers. Read the list of what you want to buy.
   - Think about what you will say.

2. **Do the shopping role play with your classmates.**

interact with peers in role play

Writing: punctuating speech

1 Read the conversation and answer the questions.

"Hello, Adu here," said Adu.
"Hello, Adu. Is Bella there?" asked Emma.
Adu answered, "No, I'm sorry. She's just gone shopping."

1. Where do we put speech marks?
2. Which kind of punctuation mark do we use at the end of speech?
3. How do we show who is speaking? Which verbs do we use? Which other verbs could we use?

2 Write the rest of the conversation between Adu and Emma. Use speech marks and the correct punctuation marks and verbs.

EMMA

Is she at the mall?

ADU

No, she had to go to the supermarket to get food for tonight.

OK. Please ask her to call me.

I will do.

My learning

We learn by doing and then by thinking about what we have done.

Think about the conversation you wrote.

How can you make it better?

Writing: a conversation

1 Work in pairs: one shop owner and one shopper from the role play. Write one of your conversations.

- Start with a short introduction: *A customer goes into …*
- Don't forget the greetings: *"Good morning / afternoon."*   *"Can I help you?"*
- Customer asks: *"I'm looking for …"*   *"Do you have …?"*
- Shopkeeper helps: *"I have … but I don't have …"*   *"What about this …?"*
- Anything else: *"How much is that?"*   *"It's …"*
   "Can you tell me …?"   *"Can you give me …?"*
- End with a short conclusion: *"Thank you. Goodbye!"*   *"Thank you for your help."*

2 Read and check your conversation.

- Is it clear who is speaking?
- Is the punctuation correct?
- Is the spelling correct? (Use a dictionary, if necessary.)

punctuation; write a dialogue

Focus on the World

Markets: three of the best

Kejetia Market, Kumasi, Ghana

The biggest market in West Africa, and one of the biggest in the world, is in Kumasi. You can buy food, clothes, anything you need for your house or car, and just about anything else – but you might need help to find it! The market has more than 11 000 shops and stalls, with about 45 000 people working there, and you can easily get lost. Ask to look at some material – the different colours are amazing!

Grand Bazaar, Istanbul, Turkey

This is one of the oldest markets in the world. It was built in 1461. It is like a small town, with 60 streets, 3000 stores, banks, restaurants and a police station. Each day up to 400 000 people visit to do their shopping or just to look around.

Cai Rang, Mekong River, Vietnam

On some of the big rivers in Asia, people do their shopping on boats. One of the biggest floating markets is Cai Rang in Vietnam. The best way to get there is by boat. It sells many products but mostly fruit and vegetables. Sellers put an example of what they are selling on the top of a long stick, to help shoppers find what they are looking for. So if you want carrots, look out for a carrot in the air! The market also has floating restaurants and other shops.

1. Which of these three markets would you most like to visit? Why?
2. Find Ghana, Turkey and Vietnam on a map or in an atlas. Look for Kumasi, Istanbul and the Mekong River.

read extended non-fiction

3 Find the words in the text. Read carefully and choose the correct meaning.

1 stall (Kejetia market)
   a a small shop (or just a table) where products are sold in a market
   b a small place to keep an animal (for example, a horse)
2 material (Kejetia market)
   a a place in a market where you can rest
   b something from which you make clothes, curtains and other things
3 floating (Cai Rang)
   a something sitting on top of water
   b moving through the air
4 stick (Cai Rang)
   a a type of boat used in Vietnam
   b a long, thin piece of wood

4 Find the words *seller* and *shopper* (Cai Rang). Study the example and answer the questions.

A farmer is someone who farms. A driver is someone who drives.

1 What is a seller?
2 What is a shopper?

5 Read what Kim is saying. Then write a short description of your favourite shopping experience. Follow the instructions below.

Hello! I'm Kim and I sometimes help my family at the floating market. We grow fruit and vegetables on our farm, and then we sell them at the market.

Where do you go shopping? Can you tell me something about the shops where you live? A picture would be nice, too.

- Choose a market, a mall, a specialist shop or any other store you like.
- Describe what it sells.
- Say who goes there.
- Explain what you like about it.
- Include any interesting facts you know about it.
- If you can, find and use a photo.

read extended non-fiction; write a description

Project: shopping experiences

In this project you are going to work in groups to consider the advantages and disadvantages of different kinds of shops.

1 Do you know what a *hypermarket* is? Read to find out.

> Some countries have hypermarkets. These are very big supermarkets, which sell almost everything. They are usually outside towns or cities and they have huge car parks for customers. It is sometimes easier to get to these hypermarkets than to get to malls because of lots of traffic in cities. Hundreds of thousands of customers use hypermarkets, so they can sell their products cheaper than most other shops.
>
> However, some people don't like hypermarkets. When lots of people visit them, there can be traffic problems in the area. People who don't have cars often cannot easily get to them. Also, hypermarkets can take customers away from shops in the cities and make it more difficult for them to make money.

2 Discuss.

Have you been to any hypermarkets? What do you think of them?

3 The text talks about some of the *advantages* (the good things) and the *disadvantages* (the bad things) of hypermarkets. Copy and complete the table.

Advantages	Disadvantages
+ [1] ___ almost everything	– make [4] ___ problems
+ easy to get to	– need a [5] ___ to get there
+ big car [2] ___	– hurt shops in the [6] ___
+ [3] ___ than other shops	

4 In your group, choose one type of shop from page 18.

1 Create a table like the one in section 3 above. Discuss and list the advantages and disadvantages.

2 Write a text like the one about hypermarkets in section 1 above.
   - Write a few sentences about the advantages.
   - Write a few sentences about the disadvantages.
   - Find and use a picture to illustrate your text.

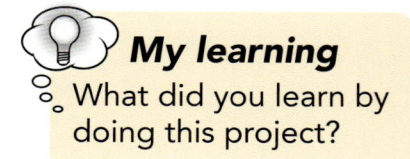

My learning
What did you learn by doing this project?

read for specific information; interact with peers; develop coherent arguments

Review 1

Speaking: looking back

Study tip
It's important to look back at what we have studied from time to time. It helps us remember. So ... it's review time!

Look back through Units 1 and 2.

1. Find one photo you like. Say why it interests you.

2. Find one activity which you enjoyed. Say why you liked it and what you learned from doing it.

Reading: a quiz

1. Work in pairs. Look through Units 1 and 2 and find the answers to these questions.
   1. What is Femi's home language?
   2. Which six feelings can everyone in the world show using their faces?
   3. How many sign languages are there?
   4. What is the name of the place where we pay in a self-service shop?
   5. How many streets are there in the Grand Bazaar in Istanbul?

2. Write five different questions about Units 1 and 2.

3. Work with another pair. Ask and answer your questions.

Writing: meeting people

Read a fact file about Joy. Imagine you meet her. Follow the instructions and write the conversation.

Name:	Joy
Nationality:	Chinese
Home language:	Chinese
Other languages:	English
Hobbies:	swimming, computer games
What she says:	"I want to travel to lots of places so I want to speak English well. It's a very useful language."

- Greet her.
- Ask her a question.
- Agree or disagree with what she says about English.
- Give your opinion about learning English.

review

Vocabulary: shopping

What are these?
1. A shop that sells only one type of product (for example, jewellery).
2. You can put this inside a watch, a camera, a phone, a toy, and so on to make it work.
3. A four-letter word that means *very big*.
4. A place where you can buy medicine, soap, shampoo, and so on (also called a chemist's).
5. The opposite of *advantage*.

Use of English: indefinite pronouns

Copy and complete the sentences with the words from the box.

| anybody | everyone | everything | nobody | someone | something |

1. Can you come here, please? I want to tell you _____ .
2. My father knows _____ about computers.
3. Has _____ seen my pen?
4. Where is _____ ? I've emailed all my friends but _____ has answered.
5. I need _____ to help me with my homework.

Use of English: correcting

Work in pairs. Find the mistake and correct it.

Can you say …?

> 1. I's just seen Amy playing tennis.   No, you should say …
> 2. Where is Flo? She hasn't came to school.   No, you should say …
> 3. Yes, she has. She's arrived just. Look!   No, you should say …
> 4. I went shopping and now I only have a few money.   No, you should say …
> 5. This classroom is not as bigger as the one next door.   No, you should say …

Catching the criminals 3

Looking forward

This unit explores crime and criminals, and how the police catch them.

You will read
- some news reports about crimes
- a blurb for a crime story
- about the science of catching criminals

You will listen
- to a police report about a crime

You will speak
- about different crimes and how serious they are

You will write
- a police report
- a blurb for a crime story

You will learn
- about using the past passive
- about reported speech

The criminal world

Speaking: what's a crime?

1 Make a list of any crimes you can name.

2 Work in pairs. Discuss which of these sentences you think describes a crime.
- Adam takes $100 from the bag of someone sitting next to him on a bus.
- Betty buys a book that costs $10. She gives the seller $20. He gives her $40 back. She says nothing and leaves the shop.
- Cal parks his car where he shouldn't park.
- Danni is a waitress. Her boss pays her very little. She takes some food home for her children.
- Ed finds his father's password and uses it to go into his father's computer and buy some computer games.
- Freda uses her computer to get information from other people's computers. She uses it to get their money.
- Greg goes out to sea and takes ships from people. He asks for money to return the ships.
- Hina is the boss of an oil company. The company puts dirty water into a river. Some children become ill after swimming in the river.

3 With your partner, order the crimes from the most serious (**1**) to the least serious (**8**).

1 …

4 Discuss your answers with another pair.

Vocabulary: crimes

1 Which types of criminal are the people described in question **2** above?

| computer hacker | pirate | thief |

1 Adam is a …
2 Freda is a …
3 Greg is a …

2 Read about a car thief. Work in pairs to make sure you understand the meaning of all the underlined words. Use a dictionary, if necessary.

Ivan <u>breaks into</u> a car and <u>steals</u> it. A <u>police officer</u> stops Ivan and <u>arrests</u> him. Ivan finds a <u>lawyer</u> to help him at his <u>trial</u>. He is sent to <u>prison</u> for three months.

give and discuss opinions; vocabulary of crime

Reading: setting the scene

Read these headlines for some newspaper reports. What do you think the reports will be about?

TEENAGE HACKER ARRESTED

Celebrity car thief trial starts

SIX MONTHS FOR TEA-DRINKER

PIRATES CATCH FISHING BUSINESSMAN

Reading: exploring the text

1 Read the newspaper reports. Match them to the headlines above.

a
When Mr and Mrs Elba arrived home from holiday, they were surprised to find a man sleeping on their sofa. Mr Elba offered the thief a cup of tea while his wife called the police.

Officers arrived to find the three of them drinking tea at the kitchen table.

Yesterday, the lawyer for the man, Jo Jones, said that nobody was hurt and nothing was stolen so there was no crime. However, Jones was sent to prison for six months.

b
Police arrested a 15-year-old girl at her home early yesterday morning. Reports say that the teenager's computer was also taken.

This follows reports of a hack into the Highlands School computer. Information about many teachers and students was posted on social media.

c
Police are today looking for businessman Ali Modi. He was fishing on his boat yesterday when he was taken away by pirates.

Mr Modi's wife has offered a reward of $200 000 to anyone who can find her husband.

d
The trial of Ivan Conti for stealing a car from celebrity singer Angela Hope started today.

A police officer read a report of what happened.

It described Conti driving Miss Hope's car fast when it was seen by two police officers. When the car was stopped, police found a laptop, a box of mobile phones and a woman's handbag in the car.

2 Study the newspaper reports and answer these questions.

1. Do the reports have short or long paragraphs?
2. Do the reports give facts or opinions?
3. Are the headlines short or long?

read for main points; typical features of newspaper reports

Reading: understanding the text

Look again at the newspaper reports on page **31**. Are these sentences *true*, *false* or the report *doesn't say*?

1 Jo Jones broke into the Elbas' home.
2 Jo Jones isn't a criminal.
3 The girl hacker is a student at Highlands School.
4 Ali Modi is fishing today.
5 Ali Modi's wife wants help to find him.
6 Police think Ivan Conti stole a car.

Vocabulary: words in context

1 In the report about the pirates and Ali Modi, find:
  a a word that means some money given to someone for help to find something or someone.

2 In the report about the trial of Ivan Conti, find words that mean:
  a someone who is famous, usually on TV, in films or pop music.
  b a description of what happened.

Use of English: the passive

1 Read and compare the A and B sentences about the crimes. Answer the questions.

> *Language tip*
> We often find passives in reports.

A Ali Modi <u>was taken</u> by pirates.
B Pirates <u>took</u> Ali Modi.

A Mr and Mrs Elba <u>were surprised</u> by a man sleeping on the sofa.
B A man sleeping on the sofa <u>surprised</u> Mr and Mrs Elba.

1 The A and B sentences have the same meaning. One is active and one is passive. Which is which?
2 Look at the verbs. They are all in the past tense. How do we form the past passive?

   ____ or ____ + past participle

2 Read the sentence and answer the questions.

   Information was posted on social media.

1 Does the sentence tell us *who* posted the information?
2 How can you write this as an active sentence?

3 Find other examples of passives in the reports. Do they use *by …*?

read for specific information; passives

Police reports

Speaking: a strange robbery

Read about what happened last weekend. Work in pairs to write a report using the passive.

Last weekend some people broke into the zoo. They stole a monkey. Then they took a penguin. They put the animals into a car. Somebody heard the noisy animals at the zoo and called the police. The police arrested the thieves. Happily, nobody hurt the animals.

> **Did you know …?**
> You can search online to find a list of irregular past participles. You can also look up a verb in a dictionary, and it will tell you the past tense and the past participle if it is an irregular verb.

Listening: a police report

1. 🔊 Listen to a police report. Which one of the four newspaper reports on page 31 is it about?

2. Listen again and look at the picture of the car. Letters A–C show where the three objects that the police found were. What were the objects?

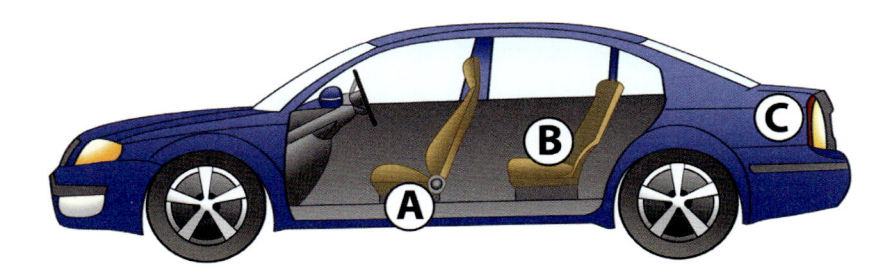

Listening: exploring the text

What information does the report include?

- Does it tell us …

    when (time and date)?
    where (address)?
    who (name of person / people)?
    what (the police saw / happened)?
    why (reasons for the crime)?

- Does it give …

    facts (things that are true)?
    opinions (ideas about things)?
    suggestions (what to do next)?

- Is the report …

    formal or **informal**?

passives; listen for specific information; features of formal reports

Use of English: reported speech

1 **Compare the police report with what Angela Hope actually said. Then complete the rules.**

She said that there was a man outside in her car.

> There is a man outside in my car.

She said that he was driving away fast.

> He is driving away fast.

When we report what Angela Hope said, we

- start with: **She _____ that …**
- change pronouns: "*… in my car*" changes to **in _____ car**.
- change verb tense: "*There is …*" changes to **there _____ …**

  "*… he is driving …*" changes to **he _____ driving …**

2 **What did the people say?**

1. The teacher said that someone had hacked the school computer.

   > Someone …

2. Mrs Modi said that she had offered $200 000 to help find her husband.

   > ?

3. Mrs Elba said that there was a man their house.

   > ?

4. She said that her husband was making tea for him.

   > ?

3 **Report what the man said.**

1. There's a robbery! — A man said that …
2. Two men have broken into the bank. — He said that …
3. Another one is outside in a car. — …
4. It's my car. They've just stolen it. — …

34   *reported speech*

Writing: a report

1 Copy and complete the table about a crime.

When?	
Where?	
Who?	
What?	

2 Imagine you are a police officer. Write a report about the crime.
- Use formal language.
- Give the facts. Don't give opinions.
- Use passives when you don't know who did something:

    The bank's computer was hacked at 18.00 on Tuesday 27th September.
- Use reported speech:

    Mr Rajif said that he was at home when the thieves took his car.

3 In groups, take turns to read out your reports.

Writing: checking punctuation and spelling

1 Look at the example sentences in section **2** above.
  1. How many capital letters are there? For each one, say why a capital letter is used.
  2. Find an apostrophe ('). Why is it used?

2 Check the punctuation in your report. Have you used full stops and capital letters correctly?

3 Check your report for correct spelling. Use a dictionary, if necessary.

4 Now write your report again and try to make it better.

> **My learning**
> Think about the report you wrote and read out. What did your friends say when you read it out?
>
> Did you get the spelling and punctuation correct? How could you make your report better?

write a report with appropriate style and register; spelling and punctuation

Focus on Science

Science: finding evidence

Forensic science uses different types of sciences (for example, biology, chemistry) to look for answers about crime and criminals. It's a bit like a game. It involves working out a **puzzle** to **solve** the **mystery** of what happened at a **crime scene**. For example, forensic science can help to show that a person was at the scene of the crime when it happened (even if that person says they were somewhere else).

Fingerprinting has been an important part of forensic science for over a hundred years. Everyone's fingerprints are different; no two fingerprints are the same. After a crime, forensic scientists **search** the crime scene for fingerprints and **compare** them with the fingerprints of **known** criminals.

More recently, forensic scientists have found a new and more useful tool – DNA.

A *fingerprint*

DNA is easier than fingerprints to find because we can get DNA from almost anything a person might leave behind. DNA can be found in blood, in hair and even in **tears**.

Not all crimes happen in the real world. Something that is happening more and more often is that computers are used by criminals. However, computers are also a great place to find **clues** to help solve crimes. If a computer is used to steal **data** from another computer, forensic scientists can **examine** the computer and find **evidence** that can bring criminals to trial.

What is DNA?

Well, its full name is *deoxyribonucleic acid*, and it contains the information that makes every one of us what we are. DNA, along with the information it contains, is passed from adults to their children, and is different for everyone.

What is DNA profiling?

A few drops of blood or one hair found at a crime scene is enough to develop a DNA **profile**. Forensic scientists can compare this profile with the profiles of other people to see if they **match**. If two DNA profiles are the same, there can only be a one-in-a-billion chance that the DNA is from two different people.

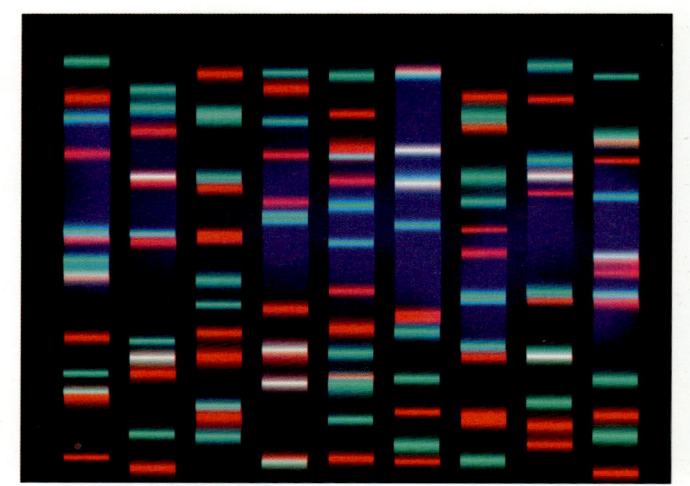

Part of a DNA profile

read extended non-fiction

1 **Discuss what you know before you read.**

How can science help the police catch criminals?

2 **Read the text section by section to understand the main points. Then answer the questions.**

1. What is forensic science? Read the first paragraph of the text to find out.
2. Paragraphs 2 and 3 introduce the two most important tools for forensic scientists. What are these tools?
3. Paragraph 4 introduces a new kind of crime. What is it?
4. The information box is about DNA. Which of the following does it tell us about?
   a what the letters DNA stand for   b what DNA is
   c when DNA was found   d how forensic scientists use DNA

3 **Read the text again to understand new words.**

1. Copy and complete the sentences using words in **bold** in paragraph 1.
   a Sometimes problems are very difficult to _____, so you need help with them.
   b The police arrived at the _____ very quickly and stopped everyone walking over it.
   c When I get home, I like to play a difficult game or find the answer to a _____ on my computer.
   d I don't understand why you stopped playing tennis. It's a _____ to me because you were very good.
2. Find words in **bold** in paragraph 2 that mean the following:
   a to look carefully to find something
   b to look carefully to see how people or things are the same or different
   c somebody or something we already know about.
3. Paragraph 3 tells us that DNA is found in blood, hair and tears. What are **tears**?
4. Match these words in **bold** from paragraph 4 with their meanings.

1 clues	a a piece of information that makes you believe something is true
2 data	b information stored on a computer
3 examine	c information that helps you find an answer
4 evidence	d to look at carefully

5. Find words in **bold** in the DNA information box that mean the following:
   a a description of someone   b to be the same as something else

4 **Discuss.**

Would you like to be a forensic scientist? Why / Why not?

read extended non-fiction; read for specific information   37

Project: blurb for a crime story

In this project you are going to work in pairs to write the blurb for a crime story of your own.

A blurb is a short description of a book, to encourage someone to read it.

1 Read the blurb for *Appointment with Death* and answer the questions.
   1. What does the blurb tell us about the author?
   2. What does it tell us about the main character?
   3. What does it tell us about the setting (where the story takes place)?
   4. What does it tell us about the plot (what happens in the story)?
   5. How does it make the story sound exciting?

> **Appointment with Death**
>
> *Another exciting story from the 'queen of crime', Agatha Christie.*
>
> Mrs Boynton, a woman nobody likes, dies in the ancient city of Petra. Was she ill, was it too much sun that killed her, or has something worse happened?
>
> The great detective Hercule Poirot has some useful information, but is it enough? He has 24 hours to solve the mystery.

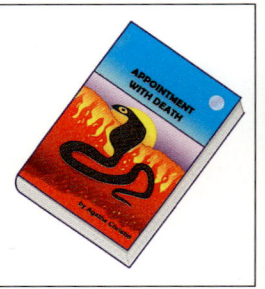

2 Work in pairs. Write a blurb for a crime story of your own.
   1. Answer these questions to plan your story. Write only the main points.
      - Main character (Who is he / she? What does he / she do?)
      - Setting (Where does the story take place?)
      - Plot (What is the crime? What happens?)
   2. Read how to write a good blurb.

   My learning
   What did you learn by doing this project?

   > **Tips for writing a good blurb**
   >
   > Be sure to include the following (in any order):
   > - the title of the story
   > - the name of the author (and maybe other famous books by the same author)
   > - the name of the main character and what kind of work he / she does (for example, *the famous detective, brilliant scientist*)
   > - where the story takes place
   > - a short explanation about what happens to make the reader interested
   > - one or two questions to the reader to make them think and want to read the story, for example: *Could it be true? What will happen next?*

   3. Write the blurb. Remember, you want to encourage people to read your crime story.

read for opinion and typical features; write with appropriate style and register

Dragons 4

Looking forward

This unit explores stories about dragons, as well as some real animals that are called dragons.

You will read
- about Komodo dragons
- about Chinese New Year celebrations
- a folk tale about a dragon

You will listen
- to a story about a monster

You will speak
- about dragons and describe them
- about some dragon-like animals
- to retell a story

You will write
- a webpage about a dragon-like animal
- about a festival

You will learn
- to talk about the unfinished past using the present perfect tense
- to talk about possibility and ability
- to report speech using *told*

Dragons: fact or fiction?

Speaking: what do you know about dragons?

Discuss.
- What stories or films do you know that have dragons in them? What do the dragons do?
- Which of these adjectives do you think can describe dragons? Use a dictionary, if necessary.

amazing	awesome	beautiful	dangerous
fantastic	friendly	huge	pleasant
strange	wonderful		

- Which other adjectives can describe dragons?
- Do you think dragons are *good* or *bad*? Why do you think this?
- Do you think dragons ever existed?

Reading: setting the scene

Are dragons real? Well some certainly are – Komodo dragons.

Look at the photo. Discuss what you know about these animals.
- How big are they?
- What do they eat?
- Where do they live?

Reading: exploring the text

1 Read to find the answers to the questions in *Reading: setting the scene*.

2 Where does the text come from?
- a   a newspaper
- b   a website for young readers
- c   a school science textbook

3 Why did the author write the text?
- a   to teach scientists about Komodo dragons
- b   to warn tourists that Komodo dragons are dangerous
- c   to interest readers in animals and nature

give opinions; use adjectives

Komodo dragons

Are dragons real? Well, some certainly are *called* dragons – Komodo dragons.

They are a type of lizard but they are nothing like the little lizards you see on walls or rocks – these ones are the largest in the world. These creatures can be three metres long and weigh 140 kilograms.

Komodo dragons are also killers. They have 60 short, sharp teeth and eat meat. They usually wait behind a tree for an animal (or even a child!) to walk past, and then they try to catch it. If the animal escapes, the Komodo dragon will follow it for hours. The reason? The Komodo has a kind of bacteria in its mouth. So, if a Komodo bites another animal, this bacteria will kill the animal in less than 24 hours. The Komodo can then enjoy its meal. It can eat up to 80% of its body weight in one meal – that's like you eating 150 burgers in one go!

Is that a bit scary? Well, don't worry, because Komodo dragons live on just five islands in Indonesia, so you probably won't meet one! This kind of lizard has lived for millions of years in Indonesia, but they were only seen for the first time by man in 1916.

Back to Lizards for kids.

> **Fun facts**
>
> A lizard is a type of a reptile.
> A Komodo dragon lays 30 eggs at a time.

> **Word help**
>
> bacteria – very small living things, and some of them can make people ill
>
> reptile – one of a group of animals that have cold blood

Reading: understanding the text

Copy and complete the table with facts from the text.

Animal fact file

Name	Komodo dragon
Type of animal	
Where found	
Size	
Food	
Interesting facts	

read for main points; typical features of web-based information texts

Vocabulary: words in context

1 Copy and complete these dictionary entries. Study carefully the example sentences to write the correct form of the word.

1
_____ verb (bit, bitten)
to use your teeth to cut into or through something: *Komodo dragons _____ animals they want to kill.*

2
_____ noun
a living thing that is not a plant: *The _____ can be three metres long.*

3
_____ verb
to manage to get away from someone, something or somewhere: *Some animals _____ from the Komodo dragon.*

4
_____ verb
to have your home in a place: *Komodo dragons _____ in parts of Indonesia.*

5
_____ adjective
something that makes you afraid; frightening: *Komodo dragons are _____ animals because they can kill people.*

6
_____ adjective
very thin and can cut through things: *A Komodo dragon's _____ teeth can cut through meat.*

2 Complete these dictionary entries for two words with a similar meaning.

1 _____ verb
to measure how heavy something or someone is: *An adult Komodo dragon can _____ 140 kilograms.*

2 _____ noun
how heavy a person or thing is: *Komodo dragons eat 80% of their body _____ in one meal.*

3 Copy and complete these three questions. They all have the same meaning and the same answer.

How [1] _____ are you?

How much do you [2] _____ ?

What's your [3] _____ ?

45 kilograms

read for specific information

Use of English: the present perfect simple

1 **Look at this sentence from the text and answer the questions.**

This kind of dragon <u>has lived</u> for millions of years in Indonesia.

1 Did Komodo dragons live millions of years ago?
2 Do they live now?
3 What is the verb tense in the sentence?

2 **Copy and complete these grammar rules. Use the verb *be*.**

1 When we talk about something that started and finished in the past, we use the past simple tense:

Komodo dragons _____ in Indonesia millions of years ago.

2 When we talk about something in the present, we use the present simple tense:

Komodo dragons _____ in Indonesia now.

3 When we talk about something that started in the past and is still not finished, we use the present perfect simple tense.

Komodo dragons _____ in Indonesia for millions of years.

> *Language tip*
> We often use *for* and *since* with the present perfect when talking about the unfinished past.
>
> We use *since* when we give a point in time.
>
> *Scientists have known about Komodo dragons since 1916.*
>
> We use *for* when we give a period of time.
>
> *They have studied these strange creatures for over a hundred years.*

3 **Think of three things about you that started in the past and are still true now.**

Tell the class about them, using the present perfect and *since* or *for*.

> I've lived in the same house since I was born.

> We've been in this class for two months.

> *Did you know …?*
> Snakes can hear. They have ears on the inside of their heads.
>
> Penguins can jump two metres in the air.
>
> Elephants can smell water from five kilometres away.

Use of English: modal *can*

Work in pairs. Discuss answers to the questions.

These creatures *can* be three metres long and weigh 140 kilograms.

1 Are all the creatures this size? Or is it possible that only some of them are this size?
2 We use *can* to talk about ability (for example, *I can swim well*), as well as to talk about possibility (for example, *I can come to your party*). Look in the text on page 41 to find two examples of *can*. Are they talking about *possibility* or *ability*?
3 Look at the word that follows *can* in each sentence. Is it a noun, a verb or an adjective?
4 Do you know any interesting or surprising things that animals can do? Tell the class.

present perfect simple; modal can   43

Little dragons

Speaking: animal facts

Work in groups of three. Choose one of the *Animal fact files* each. Prepare to tell the rest of the group about your animal.

Animal fact file

Name	dragon fish
Type	fish
Where found	2000 metres deep in Atlantic Ocean
Size	male 5 cm / female 40 cm
Food	small fish
Interesting facts	males and females are very different; makes its own light to see deep under the sea

Animal fact file

Name	bearded dragon
Type	reptile
Where found	Australia
Size	up to 60 cm
Food	fruit, vegetables, small insects
Interesting facts	can change colour – gets lighter in the hot sun; can run at 15 kph; can sleep standing up

Animal fact file

Name	dragonfly
Type	insect
Where found	around the world near water
Size	from 1 cm to 12 cm
Food	small insects
Interesting facts	there are 5000 different types; has six legs but can't walk well; can fly backwards

Writing: an animal webpage

1. **Look again at the webpage about Komodo dragons. Discuss.**
   - Is the text formal? Give reasons for your answer.
   - Is it very serious? Find examples of what is not very serious.
   - What different sections does the text have?

2. **Write a webpage about one of the animals from the fact files above.**

write factual website texts with appropriate style, register and layout

A monster called Nian

Listening: setting the scene

You are going to listen to a story about a monster and three items. Look at the pictures of the three items and discuss these questions.

- What are they?
- What do you think the story will be about?

Listening: a story

1 🔊 Listen to the first part of the story and answer these questions.

- Who is the story about?
- Where does it take place?

2 Before you listen to the second part of the story, discuss these questions.

- Who is the old man?
- Why does he stay in the village?
- What will happen to him when Nian arrives?

3 Before you listen to the last part of the story, discuss these questions.

- What have the villagers learned?
- What will they do next new year?

Use of English: reported speech (*said* and *told*)

1 Look at these two sentences.
   a *The old man told the people that Nian didn't like the colour red.*
   b *The old man said that Nian didn't like the colour red.*

   1 Which sentence tells us who the old man was talking to?
   2 Why do we use *told* in sentence A but *said* in sentence B?

2 Choose the correct words to complete the rules.

   1 We use _____ when we say who somebody is talking to:
   The old man told the granny that he wanted to stay in the village.

   2 In other cases, we use _____: *The old man said that Nian had run away.*

3 Report what they say.
   1 "I don't like loud noise."   Nian …
   2 "You are going to listen to a story."   Our teacher …

Focus on Literature

Folk tales

> Folk tales are stories that people tell one another over many years. Grandparents and parents tell these stories to their children. The children tell the same stories to their children, and so on. Folk tales often teach or explain something.

1 Discuss.
- Which folk tales do you know? What happens in each story?
- In the stories you know, which of these is the most important?
  - characters – who is in the story
  - setting – when and where it takes place
  - plot – what happens

2 In the story below, the characters and the setting are introduced in the first paragraph. Read the paragraph and find out who the characters are and what the setting is.

3 The following seven items are all in the story. What are these items?

4 Now read the story. Put the seven items in the order they appear in the story.

The Dragon Stone

Long ago, there was a young boy called Nie Lang who lived with his mother in a very poor part of China. He was too poor to go to school, so he worked for the rich, cruel landowner, Zhou. Nie Lang's job was to find grass to feed Zhou's horses.

46   read extended fiction

One year there was no rain. The river was low and dirty and the land turned brown. Nie Lang couldn't find grass for the horses near his home, so one day he set out to climb Dragon Mountain. He hoped to find grass on the other side of the mountain. However, everything was the same there, it was dead or dying. Suddenly, he looked up and saw a large white rabbit looking at him. The beautiful creature wasn't afraid of Nie Lang and let him come close. It turned and walked away, then stopped to wait for the boy to follow. The rabbit led Nie Lang to a patch of beautiful green grass. Nie Lang was delighted. He cut all the grass and hurried home.

The next day Nie Lang went back over Dragon Mountain and found the same place with the help of the rabbit. To his surprise, the grass was long, thick and green once more. Again, Nie Lang went home with food for the horses. The same thing continued for several days, but then Nie Lang had an idea. The next time he visited the place, he took a spade with him. He dug up the ground around the grass so that he could take it home with him. He didn't want to have such a long walk every day. While Nie Lang was digging, he found a beautiful white stone. He took the stone home, too, and gave it to his mother. She put it in an empty rice jar in the kitchen.

The next morning, Nie Lang was very sad to see that the grass had become a dirty yellow and brown colour. He went inside to tell his mother and was amazed to find that the floor was covered with rice. Nie Lang and his mother found that the jar with the stone was full of rice, and that more rice was pouring out of it. There was enough rice for Nie Lang, his mother and all the people of the village.

Zhou, the landowner, soon heard about the magic white stone. He visited Nie Lang's house to try to take it. Nie Lang saw the landowner and his men coming, so he took the stone from the jar, put it in his mouth and swallowed it. Zhou's men smashed their furniture and ripped up all their clothes, but they weren't able to find the stone. As Nie Lang watched, he began to feel the stone moving in his stomach. And he began to feel very thirsty. He ran down to the river and began to drink and drink and drink. Something strange was happening!

Zhou was really angry. He screamed, "Where is Nie Lang?"

In reply came a deep, loud, strong voice, "Nie Lang is here. Turn and face him."

Standing in the river was a huge dragon. It slowly rose up on its back legs and water flowed off its mighty blue, red and purple body. Then, with a mighty roar, fire shot out of its mouth and burned Zhou and his men. The dragon opened its silver wings and took off into the air. As it flew, Nie Lang's mother called out 'Nie Lang' 24 times. Each time, the dragon nodded its magnificent head. A huge storm took place, and the rain brought colour back to the dry land.

Nowadays, people say the dragon Nie Lang brings rain to that part of China.

5 Find all the words for colour in the story. What do you think the descriptions of colour give to the story?

Project: a festival

In this project you are going to work in groups to find out about a festival.

1 The story on page **45** told us about the beginnings of the celebrations for Chinese New Year. Now read more about the Chinese New Year festival.

> New Year celebrations in China are a time for lots of family fun. A family prepares for the new year by cleaning their house. They then decorate their house and themselves using the colour red. Parents and grandparents give young people presents of money in red envelopes. There are special family meals and wonderful sweets for children. And there are fireworks!
>
> An exciting part of the festival is the dragon dance. Dragons are seen as bringing people good luck and long life. They believe that the dragon dance scares away bad luck. Dragons up to 100 metres long are held up on sticks, and people lift the dragon up and down so that it looks like it is dancing.

2 What does the text and photo in section **1** above tell us about the following?

- how the family prepares
- what they wear
- what they eat and drink
- what they do
- special parts of the festival

3 How does the photo help us understand the festival?

4 Work in groups. Write about another festival.

1 Choose a festival celebrated in your country or in another country. Do some research to help you choose.

2 Decide who in your group will do each part of the work:
- find and note down the information
- find the photos
- write the text
- design what your work will look like (put the writing and the photos together in an attractive way).

3 Work together to finish your project.

5 Show your project to other groups.

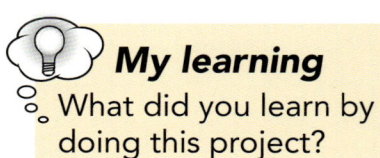

My learning
What did you learn by doing this project?

read for specific information; research, plan and compose a factual text

Review 2

Speaking: looking back

> **Study tip**
> It's time once more to look back at what we have studied. This helps us remember.

Work in groups. Look back through Units 3 and 4 and discuss these questions.

- What is your favourite photo in the units? Why do you like it?
- Which activity did you like the most? Why did you enjoy it? What did you learn from it?

Listening: what's missing?

1 Read the police report which you listened to in Unit 3. Think about how to fill the gaps 1–6.

A phone call ¹ _____ from Miss Angela Hope at 15:05 on 10th January this year. She said she was in her apartment and could see a man outside in her car. He then ² _____ fast. The car was a red Mercedes with the number AH 275.

The next day, at 11:28 on the 11th January, the car ³ _____ by police officers in the north of the city. They ⁴ _____ the car and made it stop. The driver gave his name as Ivan Conti.

The officers looked in the car and some items ⁵ _____ In a box in the back of the car, 15 mobile phones were found. All of the phones had been ⁶ _____ from a shop that morning. Under the driver's seat there was a woman's handbag. Miss Hope later said that it was her handbag. On the back seat of the car there was a laptop computer. This was also Miss Hope's.

2 🔊 Now listen and write down the missing words.

Reading: another crime

Read the text and answer the questions.

Police were called today to the National Bank in the centre of the city.

This follows reports that more than $300 000 is missing from some bank accounts. It seems that the bank's computer was used to move money to other countries.

A police officer reported that a 25-year-old bank worker was helping them at the police station.

1 Where can you find texts like this?
2 What is the crime?
3 The last sentence reports what a police officer said. Write the words that were spoken.
4 Write a headline for the report.

Writing: a police report

Complete the police report about the crime at the bank. Add any details you like. Remember that for this kind of report:

- use formal language
- give facts – don't give opinions
- use passives when you don't know who did something
- use reported speech.

A phone call was received from the National Bank at …

Vocabulary: catching a thief

Copy and complete these sentences using the words from the box.

| arrest | cruel | evidence | male | prison | solve |

1. A police officer said today that they are looking for a _____ aged about 35.
2. They are looking for the man to _____ him for theft.
3. The police said that they hoped to _____ the crime soon.
4. The thief left his DNA at the crime scene, so the police have some _____.
5. It was a very _____ crime because an old woman was hurt.
6. We all hope the man will go to _____ for a long time.

Use of English: reported speech

Can you remember the story of the monster Nian? What did the old man and the granny say?

1. I want to stay in the village.

   The old man said _____ .

2. You're in danger here.

   Granny _____ the old man _____ .

3. I'm not afraid of Nian.

   The old man _____ her _____ .

50 review

Art 5

Looking forward

This unit explores different works of art.

You will read
- a newspaper report about some problems
- about African art

You will listen
- to a description of a painting

You will speak
- about what you think of art in general, and some examples in particular
- about how rubbish can be made into art
- about a favourite work of art

You will write
- a description of a painting (including your opinion of it)

You will learn
- to use words about art
- about relative clauses
- about abstract nouns
- to use *like* and *as* in descriptions

What is art?

Speaking: is this art?

1 Discuss these questions.
- Do you like to draw or paint? Have you ever made a picture to show how you are feeling?
- What painting or sculpture have you seen that you liked? Why did you like it?

2 Discuss these statements. Which do you agree with?

Art is …

… all around us.

… useless.

… less important than science.

… made by crazy people.

… for anyone and everyone.

3 Look at the three pictures below and the picture on page 51. Discuss these questions.
- Which ones do you like? Why do you like them?
- Can each one be described as art?
- What is art?

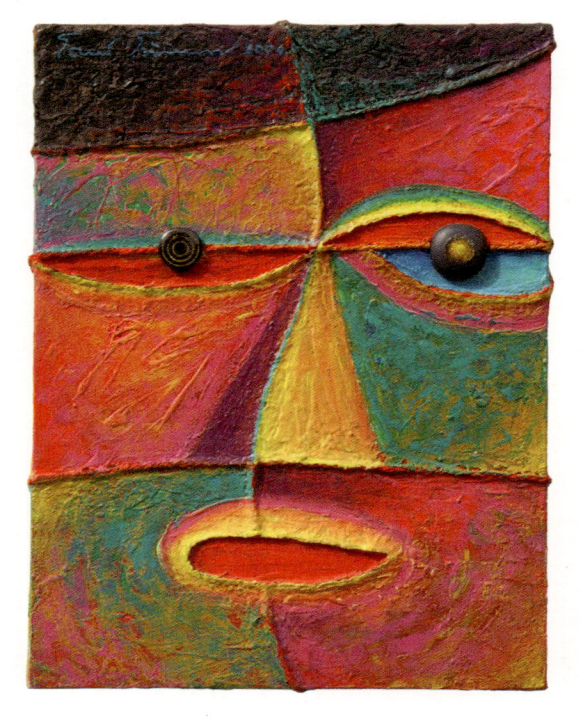

A

B

C

give opinions; respond to and discuss with others

Reading: setting the scene

Discuss these questions.

- Look at the picture. What is it?
- If you saw this in an art gallery, what would you think?

Reading: exploring the text

1 Read the newspaper report. Find answers to these questions.

1. How did the bag of rubbish get into the gallery?
2. What happened to it?

Cleaner bins rubbish bag art

A cleaner has thrown away a bag of rubbish that was part of a work of art in an exhibition at the Tate Britain gallery.

The bag, filled with used paper and other rubbish, was part of a work by Gustav Metzger. Metzger wanted to show the short life of art.

The rubbish bag was thrown away by a cleaner at the London gallery. The 78-year-old artist later replaced it with a new bag.

It is not the first time a cleaner has made such a mistake. In 2001 a cleaner, who worked at London's Eyestorm Gallery, tidied away a display by artist Damien Hirst because he thought it was a pile of rubbish.

The collection of empty bottles, coffee cups and newspapers was said to show what an artist's studio is like.

In addition, in the 1980s the work of Joseph Beuys, which included a very dirty bath, was cleaned by a gallery worker in Germany.

2 The newspaper report is about a rubbish bag at a London gallery. What else is the report about?

3 Look at the headline and answer these questions.

1. What is the verb?
2. *A rubbish bin* is a place where you put rubbish. What does the verb *bin* mean?
3. What is the subject? (*Who* binned the rubbish?)
4. Rewrite the headline as a full sentence.

Language tip

Newspaper headlines don't use full sentences. They leave out all the small words (*a, the, it, am*), and use only the most important words to show the meaning. Sometimes headlines leave out verbs (for example, *Gallery surprise, Dragon danger*).

read for gist; typical features of newspaper reports

Reading: understanding the text

Read the newspaper report again. Copy and complete the table.

Be careful! There is one box you cannot complete because the report doesn't give the answer for it. Can you guess the answer?

Event?	Where?	When?	Artist?	What happened?
A	1 _____	2 _____	3 _____	rubbish bag thrown away
B	London's Eyestorm gallery	4 _____	5 _____	6 _____
C	7 _____	1980s	8 _____	9 _____

Vocabulary: words in context

1 Copy and complete the words about art from the newspaper report.

1. e_____ — when paintings or other works of art are shown to people
2. g_____ — a room or building where works of art are shown
3. d_____ — a group of works of art put out for people to look at
4. c_____ — a group of things that someone has found or bought and put together in one place
5. s_____ — a room where an artist works

2 Match the words from the report with their meanings.

1. mistake
2. pile
3. replace
4. tidy away

a. things on top of each other
b. to get something new in the place of something that is lost
c. to take things and put them back in their place
d. something you do that is wrong

Use of English: relative clauses

1 Look at these sentences and answer the questions.

In 2001 a cleaner, <u>who worked at London's Eyestorm Gallery</u>, tidied away a display by artist Damien Hirst.

A work by Joseph Beuys, <u>which included a very dirty bath</u>, was cleaned by a gallery worker in Germany.

1. If we take out the underlined parts, are the sentences still correct?
2. Why have the underlined parts been put in the sentences?
3. Which words start the underlined parts? Why are these words not the same in both sentences?

read for specific information; relative clauses

2 Make new sentences using the information in [brackets].

1 A cleaner threw away part of a display. [he worked at Tate Britain]
2 The bag was thrown into the bins before other staff arrived at the gallery. [it was filled with rubbish]
3 Tate Britain is now one of the most popular galleries in the country. [it is in London]
4 Damien Hirst has made famous works of art from cows, sheep and sharks. [he is British]

3 Work in pairs. Make sentences of your own with relative clauses using *who* and *which*.

> Our school, which is over 50 years old, is one of the best in the country.

> Emma, who is in this class, might swim in the Olympics one day.

Language tip
We can make sentences more interesting if we add more information. We can do this by adding a relative clause to tell us more about a noun in the sentence.

Speaking: rubbish art

1 Some people make rubbish into art. Look at these pictures and discuss the questions.

A

B

- Do you like them?
- Do you think it is a good idea to make rubbish into art? Why / Why not?

2 How could you use rubbish to make a work of art? Discuss these questions.

- What would the work of art look like?
- What would you call it?
- What would it mean?

relative clauses; give opinions

What do you think about it?

Listening: setting the scene

1 Work in groups of three. Look at one of the three paintings each. Think about these questions.
- What can you see?
- What's happening?

A

B

C

2 Tell your group about the painting.

Listening: describing a painting

1 🔊 Listen. Which painting is being described?

2 Listen again. There are three parts to the talk. Match each part to one of these topics:
- a **opinion:** if the speaker likes it or not
- b **description:** what the painting looks like
- c **response:** which ideas and feelings it gives the speaker

3 What does the speaker think about the painting? Which words tell you this?

Vocabulary: abstract nouns

Read the Language tip box. Find four abstract nouns in this description of the painting.

It's a strange painting: it's like a dream. The colours are very bright but unusual. Your eye is drawn to the light bulb in the man's head and the eye in the sky. Perhaps the bulb shows thought or imagination: maybe the eye shows that we are being watched!

> *Language tip*
> Some nouns are things we can see, hear, touch, smell or feel (for example, *table, fire, computer*). We call these *concrete nouns*.
>
> Other nouns can be ideas, thoughts or feelings (for example, *love, anger, hope*). We call these *abstract nouns*.

I find it amazing. It holds my attention and makes me think but it also makes me feel uncomfortable. It is beautiful in a way but it is not an easy painting to enjoy.

Use of English: *like*

Language tip
It can help us to understand things if we compare them to something else.

1 Look again at the description of the painting on page 56. What is the painting compared to? Which word starts the comparison?

2 Make sentences with comparisons.
1. My best friend is like …   [think about your friend and other good things]
2. The noise is like …   [think about a noise and other sounds]
3. He eats like …   [think about how he eats, and something else that eats like him]

Writing: describing a painting

1 Work in pairs. Choose painting A or B to talk about.
1. Prepare to talk about the painting. Think about these questions.
   - What does it look like? What can you see? What is happening?
   - What does it make you think? How does it make you feel?
   - Do you like it? Why / Why not?

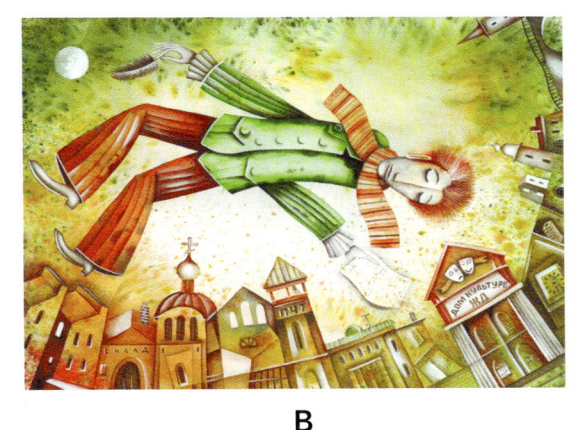

A

B

2. Tell each other about the painting.

2 Choose painting A or B to write about.

Write three short paragraphs:

1. Description (what it looks like).
2. Response (how it makes you feel).
3. Opinion (if you like it or not).

> The painting shows …   It is a scene of …
> There is / are …   The colours / shapes are …

> It's like a …   It makes me feel / think …

> In my opinion …   I think it is …
> I (don't) like it because …

preposition like; write a description with coherent structure and argument

57

Focus on Art

Art of ancient Africa

1 Match these words to their meanings. Use a dictionary, if necessary.

1	theme	a	normal (as in nature)
2	element	b	one of the different parts of something
3	performance	c	the most important idea of a piece of art or writing
4	human form	d	the shape of people
5	subject	e	the thing that is being drawn, painted, written or talked about
6	natural	f	using shapes rather than showing natural people or things
7	abstract	g	when you entertain people by singing, dancing or acting
8	cave	h	a large hole in the side of a hill or mountain

2 Choose the best words to complete this paragraph. Then answer the questions.

A **dimension** is the height, length and width of something. Some shapes on paper, like a square or a circle, have *two / three* dimensions. Real things, such as a box or a ball, have *two / three* dimensions.

1 Look at the pieces of art in the photos below. Do they have two or three dimensions?
2 Look at the piece of art in the photo on page 59. Does it have two or three dimensions?

3 Match the four types of art to the photos below.

sculpture   mask   jewellery   pottery

A   B   C   D

58 read extended non-fiction; read for main points and specific information

4 Read these six statements about ancient African art. Which statements do you think are true?

    a Most African art has three dimensions.
    b African sculptures usually show animals.
    c In the past, wearing jewellery showed how rich a person was.
    d Most African art shows people.
    e Abstract art was not used in ancient Africa.
    f The oldest art in Africa is more than 10 000 years old.

5 Read the text to find out if you were right. Correct the statements that are wrong.

Art of ancient Africa

Africa is a large continent and it has had a long history. As a result, there is a lot of different art from ancient Africa. However, much of African art has some common themes.

Three dimensions

One of the main elements of African art is that it is often created in three dimensions rather than in two dimensions. For example, sculpture was used more often than painting. These are some of the types of art from ancient Africa.

Sculpture: this was one of the most important types of art in ancient Africa. Sculptures were mostly made of people and sometimes animals.

Masks: these were an important part of African art. They were often used together with dance to create a performance.

Jewellery: many ancient African people created jewellery. It was an important part of showing how rich somebody was.

Pottery: this was used for everyday items such as bowls and cooking pots. However, some pieces of pottery were works of art, with lovely shapes and beautiful painted designs.

Human form

The subject of most African art is people. Sometimes art showed people with animals or as part-animal and part-person. Often the people in the art did not look natural, but were more abstract, with some parts of the body made strange or large, and other parts of the body left out.

Interesting facts about ancient African art

- Cave paintings found in Namibia are some of the oldest pieces of art in the world. They are more than 20 000 years old.
- Abstract African art had an influence on the modern art in Europe.

6 Which piece of African art shown in the photos do you like the most? Why?

Project: a work of art

In this project you are going to present a work of art and encourage your classmates to enjoy it.

1 Work in pairs. Find a photo of a work of art (or a real work of art) that both of you like.

The work of art can be famous or something you have made.

It can be a painting, a sculpture, or maybe …

… some pottery … a basket … or textile.

2 Write notes about your work of art. Copy and complete the table.

Type of art (for example, painting)	
Name (of your work of art)	
Description (what it looks like)	
Response (how it makes you feel)	
Opinion (why you like it)	

3 Introduce your work of art to the class. Point out the things you like about it to try to encourage them to like it too.

Did you know …?
April 15th is World Art Day. It is the birthday of Leonardo da Vinci, a famous Italian artist.

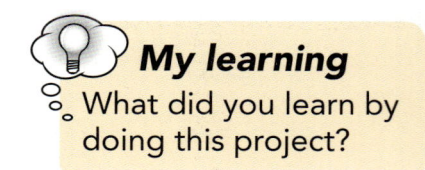

4 Write notes as you listen to other students speak.

For each work of art, note:
- the type of art
- the name of the piece
- your opinion about it.

5 Discuss.

Which was the best work of art presented to the class?

My learning
What did you learn by doing this project?

interact with peers; use appropriate language; listen for main points

Adventure sports 6

Looking forward

This unit explores some of the most exciting adventure sports.

You will read
- about some adventure sports
- the timetable for a team-building weekend
- about some national sports

You will listen
- to an interview about adventure weekends

You will speak
- about an adventure sport

You will write
- a description of an adventure sport
- your own timetable for an adventure weekend

You will learn
- about compound nouns and adjectives
- to use some conjunctions with time clauses
- to use prepositions + –ing verbs

Exploring adventure sports

Reading: setting the scene

Discuss.
- What are adventure sports? How are they different from other sports?
- Do you know what the sports are in the pictures on pages 61, 62 and 63? Can you name any other adventure sports?

A

B

Adventure sports aim to give excitement – as much excitement as possible! They are outdoor activities, not usually team sports, and have very few rules. Some of them can be dangerous.

Here are three adventure sports, sometimes called extreme sports, that are popular around the world.

Kitesurfing

In this water sport you hold on to a large kite while standing on a board. With a good wind, it's possible to surf across the sea at 100 kilometres an hour. It's also possible to jump several metres in the air and fly for 20 seconds!

Skydiving

Skydiving is when you jump from a plane and dive through the air before opening a parachute at the last minute. During the fall, skydivers enjoy the speed and seeing the world below them.

White-water rafting

This is done on small boats (called rafts) in fast-moving rivers. Where the water pours over the rocks, it becomes white, which gives the sport its name. This is one adventure sport that is not done alone – all of the people in the raft must work together as a team.

reading for gist

Reading: exploring the text

1. Read the headings and match the three sports to the pictures A, B and C.

2. Read the text again and then find the following in the pictures.

   a kite
   b parachute
   c rocks
   d board
   e raft

Reading: understanding the text

1. Choose the word to complete the sentence.

   Adventure sports are _____ [always / usually / sometimes / never] done in teams.

2. What is another name for adventure sports?

3. Which of the sports involve flying through the air?

4. What do kitesurfing and white-water rafting have in common?

5. What do you think is the most important difference between adventure sports and other sports?

Vocabulary: words in context

Find these words in the text. Then match them with their meanings.

1 aim
2 excitement
3 outdoor
4 rules
5 speed
6 pours
7 rocks

a done outside, not in a building
b how fast something moves or travels
c instructions that tell you what you can and cannot do in a sport or game
d the feeling of being excited
e to plan or hope to do something
f broken parts of the hard substance the world is made of
g when a lot of water moves fast without stopping

read for specific information

Use of English: compound words

Can you work out the names of these adventure sports?

1. Using a board to ride the waves in the sea is called *surfing*.
   a. What is surfing using a kite?
   b. What is surfing using the wind?
2. Going down a snowy mountain using two skis is *skiing*.
   What is skiing over water (behind a boat)?
3. What is going down a snowy mountain using a board?
4. Jumping into water with your arms and head first is *diving*. Swimming under water is also *diving*.
   What is jumping from a plane and diving through the sky?
5. What is biking (riding a bike) on a mountain?

> **Did you know …?**
> Names which are made of two words (for example, *skydiving*, *mountain biking*) are called **compound nouns**.
>
> A *compound adjective* is a word that describes a noun and is made up of two (or more) words. The words are joined by a hyphen (for example, *half-price*, *well-known*).

Use of English: conjunctions + time clauses

1 Look at these sentences from the text and read the Language tip box.

- … you hold on to a large kite <u>while standing on a board</u>
- … you jump from a plane and dive through the air <u>before opening a parachute</u> …

2 Now discuss the best way to complete these sentences. Use *before*, *after*, *when* or *while* and a verb in the + *–ing* form.

1. You'll be tired _____ any extreme sport.
2. A good surfer swims a long way from the beach _____ back on a wave.
3. You must think carefully about where to put your hands and feet _____ a mountain.
4. It's possible to surf at 100 kilometres an hour _____ if there's a good wind.
5. _____ for the plane to get up to 3700 metres, you jump out and skydive for about one minute.
6. _____ any dangerous sport, you must think carefully about how you can be safe.

> **Language tip**
> We can use words like *while*, *when*, *before*, *after*, *until* and *as soon as* (called **conjunctions**) to add a new section with a verb (called a **clause**) to give more meaning to a sentence.

compound nouns; conjunctions

An extreme weekend

Listening: setting the scene

Look at the advert and answer quickly.

1 What is the name of the company?
2 What does the company do?
3 If you want to know more about one of these weekends, what should you do?
4 Would you like to go on one of these weekends? Why / Why not?

Listening: an interview

You are going to listen to a reporter interviewing the manager of extremeweekends.com.

1 🔊 **Read the questions first.**

Then listen and answer.

1 Who goes on the adventure weekends?
   a families
   b groups of friends
   c families or groups of friends
2 Where do people camp?
   a on a mountain
   b next to a lake
   c next to a river
3 When can you ski?
   a every weekend   b only in winter   c when you go up the mountain
4 What does Amanda say is an easy sport for older people?
   a windsurfing   b mountain biking   c swimming

2 Listen again. Answer these questions.

1 Which is Amanda's favourite sport?
2 Which sport does Amanda talk about that is **not** in the advert?
3 What does the man asking the questions want to do?

---

extremeweekends.com
— the adventure weekend company

**Bored of doing the same old things?
Then you'll love our adventure weekends.**

You'll camp outdoors — in the open under the stars or in a tent. You'll cook your own food on a fire.
And in the day you'll choose from these activities:

- rock climbing
- mountain biking
- white-water rafting
- sailing
- windsurfing
- waterskiing
- underwater diving

and many more.

Some winter sports weekends offer:
- skiing
- snowboarding.

For details, see www.extremeweekends.com

listen for main points 65

Use of English: prepositions + –ing

1 Look at this sentence from the extremesports.com advert.

Bored *of* <u>doing</u> the same old things?

1 Look at the word in *italics*. What type of word is it (for example, noun, adjective)?
2 Look at the <u>underlined</u> word. What form of verb is it (infinitive, +–*ing*, –*ed*)?
3 Now complete the grammar rule:

The _____ form must be used when a verb comes after a _____.

2 Think of ways to complete the sentences. Use verbs in the –*ing* form.

I'm bored of …
I'm not interested in …
I'm very good at …
I'm thinking about …

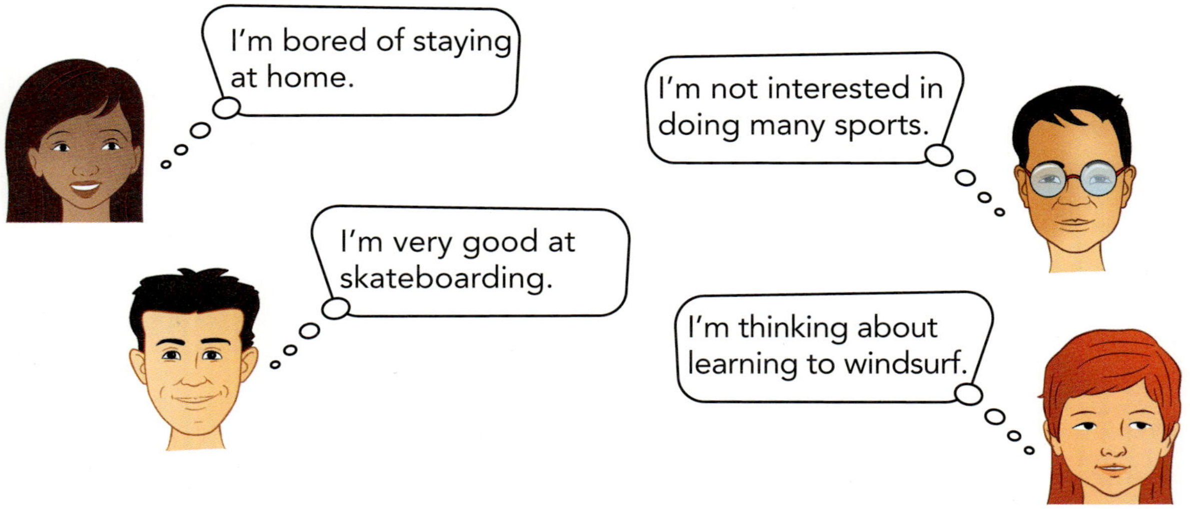

I'm bored of staying at home.

I'm not interested in doing many sports.

I'm very good at skateboarding.

I'm thinking about learning to windsurf.

listen for specific information; preposition + gerund

Which sport is it?

Writing: a description

1 Read about this sport. What is it?

> This sport is probably the most popular of all adventure sports. There may be as many as 20 million people doing it. Most of them are under 18. It started in the USA in the 1950s. People used to do it in the street and in playgrounds, but now there are many special parks where people can do this activity.
>
> It is done on a board with wheels. You need a board and should wear good trainers. You should also wear a hard hat because you can fall and hurt yourself. You must learn to do jumps and turns on the board. The best can do amazing things!

2 Write a description of an adventure sport without giving its name.

  1 Choose an adventure sport. Do some research to learn about it. Try to find some interesting facts.

  2 Look at the texts about adventure sports again. Look at the ways to introduce the descriptions.

  This sport is …   In this sport you …
  It is when you …   It is done on …

  3 Write your description.
  - Don't give the name of the sport or make it too easy to guess.
  - Make it interesting.

Speaking: presenting and discussing

Work in groups.

1 Take turns to read out your descriptions of adventure sports.

  Can you guess what they are?

2 Which is the best description in the group? Why is it the best?

Writing: editing and revising

Write your description again. It will be part of a class display.

- This time give it a title to say what the sport is.
- You can also add pictures that you find or draw.

My learning

We learn by doing and then by thinking about what we have done.

Think about the paragraph you wrote and what your friends said when you read it aloud.

How could you make it better?

compose; edit; revise a text

Focus on the World

Where can you play 'grab a goat'? Or fight to music?

How much do you know about national sports?

What's a national sport?

Simply, it's a sport that a country, or nation, chooses to be their national sport. It's not always the most popular sport in the country. In Brazil, for example, the people are crazy about football, but their national sport is a dance that looks like a fight, called *capoeira*. Brazil, like some other countries, chose a sport which is an important part of their history. *Capoeira* began in Brazil about 500 years ago.

What's my country's national sport?

Not every country has a national sport; for example, the UK doesn't have one. Others choose very popular sports, so it's no surprise that the USA has baseball as its national sport, or that Italy has football and Norway has skiing. Research online to find a list of national sports for different countries.

What other national sports are there?

Some countries, like Brazil, do things differently. For instance, the national game of Afghanistan is *buzkashi* which, in English, is 'grab a goat'. It's a game played on horses using the body of a dead goat or calf (a young cow). The aim is for one player to pick up the body quickly and carry it around before dropping it in a circle (the goal). Everyone else tries to stop the first player and do the same themselves. It doesn't really have other rules. It can be played by dozens or hundreds of horsemen (never women!). A game can last for several days.

Another traditional game which has become a national sport is *kabaddi*. This started many years ago in India and is still popular there and in other Asian countries. Since 1972 it's been the national sport of Bangladesh. It's played on a field of two halves with two teams. One member of a team has to take a deep breath, run into the other half of the field, touch one of the other team and then get back before he or she (women do play this one) breathes again!

1 **Read the text about national sports. Are these sentences true or false?**
1. The national sport of Brazil is football.
2. Every country has a national sport.
3. The national sport of the USA is baseball.
4. *Buzkashi* has a lot of rules.
5. The national sport of India is *kabaddi*.

2 **Read the text again and answer the questions.**
1. In paragraph 1, find another word for *country*.
2. In paragraph 1, *for example* is used to introduce an example about Brazil. In paragraph 3, what words are used to introduce an example about *buzkashi* in Afghanistan?
3. In paragraph 3, what is a *calf*?
4. In paragraph 3, the writer explains the game of 'grab a goat'. Which three words give the meaning of *grab*?

3 **Find these words in the text. Then match them with their meanings.**

1. fight (noun)
2. culture (noun)
3. traditional (adjective)
4. breath (noun)
5. breathe (verb)
6. touch (verb)

a. the air that goes in and out of your body
b. to take air in and out of your body
c. done in a way it has always been done
d. an activity when people hit each other
e. to put your hand or other part of your body on somebody or something
f. for example, the music or art of a country

4 **Find all the countries in the text on a map of the world.**

5 **Look at the title and headings. Why do you think the writer used questions?**

6 **Discuss. Does your country have a national sport?**
- If so, what is it? Do you think it is the best choice? What else could it be?
- If not, what sport do you think it should be? Why?

7 **Write a new paragraph for the text with the heading:**
What's the best national sport for us?

understand main points in extended non-fiction

Project: a timetable

In this project you are going to work in groups to organise an adventure weekend.

Welcome to your team-building weekend. Together we're better!

FRIDAY EVENING
- Arrive 17.00–18.00
- Put up your tent and prepare the camp.
- Light a fire, cook, eat and relax together.

SATURDAY MORNING
Bridge building
- Make a plan and then collect what you need.
- Build your bridge across the 5 m wide River Bee.

SATURDAY AFTERNOON
CHOOSE EITHER
White-water rafting
- We drive you up the mountain, you raft back down.
- Can you work together to stay inside the boat?

OR

Paintballing
- Work as a team to shoot another group with balls of paint.
- One of our most popular activities.

SATURDAY EVENING
Quiz
- 100 questions to answer and problems to solve.
- Which team knows the most?

SUNDAY MORNING AND AFTERNOON
Team sports day
- Choose from football, basketball, baseball, hockey, rugby and more.
- Each game will be part of a competition to find the top teams.

SUNDAY EVENING
Party
- Don't worry – we'll plan this for you!
- Leave 22:00.

1 Look at the timetable for a team-building weekend.
  1. What is team building?
  2. Who do you think goes on team-building weekends?
  3. Would you like to go on this weekend? Why / Why not?

2 Organise an adventure weekend for extremeweekend.com. Work in a group.
  1. Decide what activities to include, and when to do them.
  2. Make a timetable with short descriptions of the activities.
  3. You can give more than one activity for people to choose from (use *Either … Or …*).

interact to complete a group task

Review 3

Study tip
It's review time again!

Speaking: looking back

Look back through Units 5 and 6 and discuss these questions.
- Which activity did you enjoy the most? Say why you liked it and what you learned from doing it.
- Find one photo you like. Say why you like it.

Reading: a quiz

1 Work in pairs. Find the answers to these questions in Units 5 and 6.
  1 What was the name of the artist who put a bag of rubbish in a display at Tate Britain?
  2 What different types of art can you name?
  3 How many dimensions does a sculpture use?
  4 What do we call a noun that is made of two words, for example: *bathroom*.
  5 What is the national sport of Italy?

2 Write five more questions to ask about Units 5 and 6.

3 Work with another pair. Ask and answer your questions.

Writing: describing a picture

Describe the painting. Write sentences to answer the questions.
- What can you see? What are the people doing?
- What does it make you think? How does it make you feel?
- Do you like it? Why / Why not?

Vocabulary: extreme sports

What are these sports?
1 It's done on a mountain with snow. You need two skis to do this sport.
2 You also use skis for this sport. It's done on the water and it's not done on snow. You need a boat to pull you.

review 71

3 You need a board with wheels. You don't need a kite or a parachute.
4 It's a water sport. You do it on a raft in a river. You don't do it on the sea.
5 You use a kite and a board to move fast on the sea.

Vocabulary: compound nouns

1 Match words from each balloon to make the names of six sports.
Be careful! Are they one word (*snowboarding*) or two words (*mountain biking*)?

foot
mountain
rock
sky
snow
wind

diving
biking
boarding
surfing
ball
climbing

2 Write a description for each of the six sports. Use a dictionary, if necessary.

Use of English: correcting

Work in pairs. Find the mistake and correct it.
Can you say …?

1
The Louvre, who is in Paris, is an art gallery.
No, you should say *which is in Paris*.

2
A cleaner threw away part of a display, who worked at Tate Britain.
No, you should say …

3
The painting is as a dream.
No, you should say …

4
Are you interested in learn French?
No, you should say …

The future of transport

7

Looking forward

This unit explores many different forms of transport, both present and future.

You will read
- an infographic about green cars
- about a new type of train

You will listen
- to a news report about a famous flight

You will speak
- about forms of transport
- about the future of transport
- about traffic problems and solutions

You will write
- an infographic about a new train
- part of an infographic about the future of transport

You will learn
- about some conjunctions
- about different ways to talk about the future
- some transport words

Transport: old and new

Speaking: word race

1 What do these photos all have in common?

2 Work in groups. List all the types of transport you can think of in two minutes. Which group has the most?

3 Discuss. How can you divide your transport words into separate groups?

Listening: setting the scene

1 Look at the photo. Discuss.
- What do you know about the plane?
- What is special about it?
- Why was it built?

2 Listen to a news report about the plane.

Solar Impulse 2 in flight

- What have you learned about the plane and its flight now?

Listening: the future is here

1 Listen once more to the news report about *Solar Impulse 2*. Complete the sentences on page 75 with a word or short phrase.

interact with peers; vocabulary of transport

The flight began and ended in Abu Dhabi, and took ¹ _____ months from start to finish. The whole journey was about ² _____ kilometres.

The plane is very light but is big and slow. It only has the power of a ³ _____ and flies at around 75 kilometres per hour. Because of this, it took ⁴ _____ to fly across the Pacific Ocean.

Since all the plane's power comes from ⁵ _____, it didn't use any fuel on the journey. This shows that it is possible to fly without fuel! On arrival, the pilot said, "The future is ⁶ _____, the future is ⁷ _____, the future is ⁸ _____.

2 What do you think the pilot meant when he talked about the future?

  a Young people must take over now and make the future clean.
  b It is possible to have a clean future, so we must make it start now.
  c The future has started now, so we must all be clean.

Vocabulary: words in context

Find nouns in the text above that mean the following:
1 the strength of something
2 something that is used to give heat or power
3 when you arrive somewhere.

> **Did you know …?**
> *Solar* means 'from the Sun', so *solar power* means power from the Sun.

Use of English: conjunctions *as*, *since*

1 Look at these two sentences from the listening text.

Both sentences give a *reason* (why something happens) and a *result* (what happens).

A	B
As it only flies at around 75 kilometres per hour,	it took five days and five nights to fly across the Pacific Ocean.
Since all its power comes from the Sun,	it didn't use any fuel on the journey.

1 Which part (A or B) gives the reason? Which part gives the result?
2 Which words start the reason clause?
3 Can you think of another word that could start the reason clause?

2 Think of ways to finish these sentences.

- As we now know that planes can fly without fuel, …
- Since we want to keep the world clean, …
- As I went to bed early last night, …
- Since I want to do well at school, …

Green cars

Reading: setting the scene

1 Read these dictionary entries. Do you know what the words are?

Use a dictionary to check your answers.

1 _____ **noun**

the natural world of land, the seas, the air, plants and animals

2 _____ **verb**

to make air, water or land dirty and dangerous

3 _____ **uncountable noun**

the process of making air, water or land dirty and dangerous

2 How do cars and other vehicles pollute the environment?

3 What do you think *environmentally friendly* means?

4 What is an environmentally friendly car?

Reading: exploring the text

1 Look at the text on page 77. In what ways is it different from the text on page 80?

2 Read the Language tip box. What do you think an *infographic* is?

3 Read the text on page 77. Explain what it is about in one sentence.

> *Language tip*
> The text on page 77 is an *infographic*. Infographic is a word made from two other words: *information* and *graphic*. A graphic is a drawing or a picture (often produced by a computer).

Reading: understanding the text

Discuss in groups.

1 Imagine that you have an electric car.
   a   What must you do to get power into the car's battery?
   b   What happens after driving for a few hundred kilometres?
   c   What could solve the problem with electric cars?

2 In what way is a hybrid car environmentally friendly? In what ways is it not?

3 In what ways are hydrogen cars and electric cars similar? In what ways are they different?

4 A plane has been able to use solar power to fly all around the world. Why do you think solar cars are not able to produce enough power to work for very long?

use a dictionary; features of infographic; read for detail of an argument

What are green cars?

They are cars that are environmentally friendly because they make little, or no, pollution. All cars need fuel. Most cars use petrol or diesel. When these fuels burn in the car's engine, they pollute the air. It is not healthy for people to breathe in polluted air.

Electric cars

Electric engines do not pollute the air and can work well. However, they need a battery to hold the electricity that makes the car work. The problem is to make a battery that is not too big or heavy and that will hold enough power to make the car move. At the moment, electric cars are only able to travel for a few hundred kilometres. Then you have to plug them in to a source of electricity to get more power to the battery.

Hybrid cars

Hybrid means a mix of two things, and so hybrid cars are a mix of electric cars and petrol cars. If there is no power in the car's battery, it is able to continue to travel using the petrol engine.

Hydrogen cars

These also have an electric engine, but the power is made using hydrogen. The car has to carry the hydrogen.

Solar cars

These cars have solar panels in their roofs. At the moment, these types of cars cannot produce enough power to be able to travel for long. However, the solar panels can help a car travel using less petrol, so they are able to reduce pollution.

The future?

What type of cars will we be using in the future? Maybe it will be one of these four types – or maybe something new. So the future is not now, but it is going to be clean (or cleaner than now).

read for specific information

Vocabulary: words in context

1 Match the words from the text on page **77** with their dictionary meanings.

1	burn	a	to connect something to the electricity supply
2	plug in	b	to make
3	a mix	c	to make less
4	continue	d	to not stop
5	produce	e	to create fire to make power in an engine
6	reduce	f	two or more things mixed together

2 Copy and complete these sentences with words from the text.
1. Petrol and diesel are types of _____ .
2. All vehicles need an _____ to make them move.
3. Electric cars need a big _____ to hold the power so that they can move.

Use of English: the future

1 Look at the final section of the text on page **77**. Find two different forms for talking about the future.

2 Discuss.
- Which form is used to talk about something for which we have evidence?
- Which form is used to talk about a prediction or a guess? Which word tells us that the writer is not sure?

3 Work in pairs. Decide how to complete the sentences.
- Use *[be] going to* if there is some evidence.
- Use *will* if it is a prediction.

1. Car companies are working hard, so green cars _____ be better soon.
2. In 2030, most people _____ probably drive environmentally friendly cars.
3. I hope my father _____ buy a green car soon.
4. My father says he's been looking at green cars and he _____ buy a hybrid one.

Speaking: the future of transport

Discuss.
- Is transport going to be more environmentally friendly?
- How do you think people will travel to school and work in the future?
- What new forms of transport will there be?

Maglev trains

Writing: an infographic

1 Read about a new form of rail transport.

> Maglev trains are a new and exciting environmentally friendly form of transport. They are also very high speed. Magnets are used to lift the train off the rails, and then to move them over the rails. This means that they can move faster than normal trains but using less power. The power for the magnets comes from electricity, so no pollution from normal fuels is created. A Maglev train in Japan has travelled at 600 kilometres an hour. This is three times faster than normal trains.

2 Work in pairs. Rewrite the information to complete the infographic.

- Give the infographic a short title.
- Write short sentences for each of the four boxes. Include only the key information.
- Use fewer than 15 words for each box. Write no more than 50 words in total.

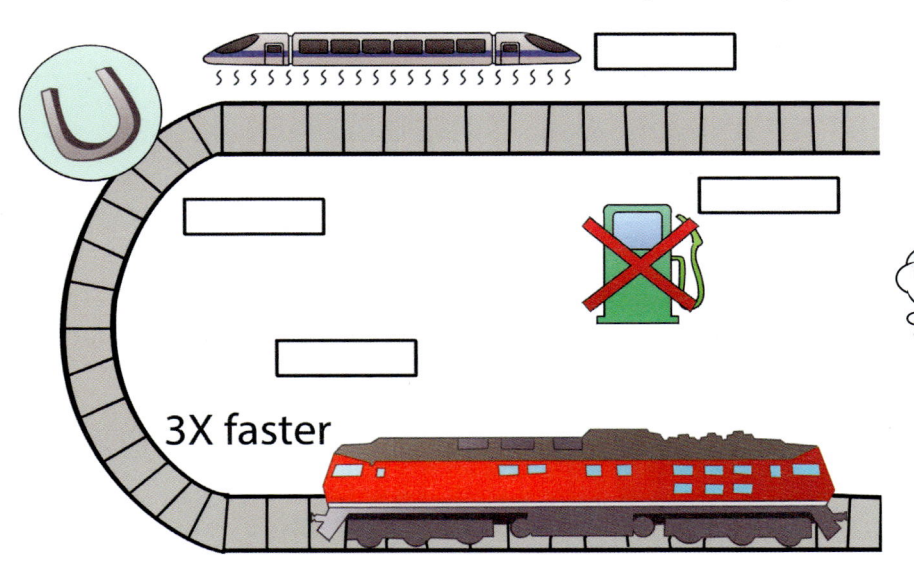

3X faster

My learning

Think about the text you have written. How many words does it have in total? Could you make it shorter and better?

write an infographic; use appropriate layout

Focus on Geography

1 These photos show some of the problems with traffic in cities. Discuss.
- What are the problems?
- What causes the problems?
- What are the solutions?

2 Read the text to find out more about the problems and their causes.

Urbanisation and traffic management

As a country develops and gets more factories, shops and businesses, the number of people living in towns and cities increases. They move from poor rural areas to urban areas where there is more employment. This process is called **urbanisation**. A **rural** area is an area of countryside. An **urban** area is a town or city.

Many developed countries are urban societies. In the UK, 90% of the population live in towns and cities. Urbanisation is something that is happening across the world.

Living in cities is not always easy. Many people choose to move out when they get the chance. They may choose to live on the edge of urban areas rather than in the centre of the city. However, they often still work, shop and drive their cars in the city centre. A lot of traffic comes together and slows down in the city centre. When the roads are full of traffic, we call it **congestion**.

Mostly, cars travel into the urban centre on large roads and motorways. They then arrive at older, smaller and narrower roads in the city centre. Congestion can be so bad that the traffic can stop altogether. We call this a **traffic jam**.

Some cities have a **traffic management plan**. They look at all the problems caused by traffic, and then create a plan that tries to solve as many problems as possible.

3 The most important new words are explained in the text. Which words are these?

4 Which other words do you need to know to understand the text? Write a list.

5 Work in groups. Discuss your lists of words.
- Help one another with the meanings of any words you already know.
- Look up the rest of the words in a dictionary (a book or online).
- Ask your teacher if you need help.

6 Work in pairs. Which of these are *problems* and which are *solutions*? Sort them into two lists.
- accidents with pedestrians (people walking and not in a vehicle)
- bypasses (roads around a town so that cars do not have to travel through the centre)
- car shares (people share a car on a journey to work and back)
- congestion
- congestion charging (pay to drive into a city centre at a busy time)
- cycle lanes (small roads where only bikes can travel)
- one-way streets (vehicles can travel in one direction only)
- park and ride (park your car outside the city and take a bus into the centre)
- parking
- pollution
- public transport (for example, buses, taxis, trains, trams)
- road accidents
- traffic jams

7 What are *pedestrian zones*? Do you think they are a good idea? Why / Why not?

8 Work in groups. What are the advantages and disadvantages of pedestrian zones for different people? Copy and complete the table.

	Advantages	Disadvantages
Shop owners		
People who live in the area		
Van and lorry drivers		
Cyclists		
Tourists		

interact with peers; use appropriate subject-specific vocabulary

Project: the future of transport

In this project you are going to complete the class infographic below about the future of transport.

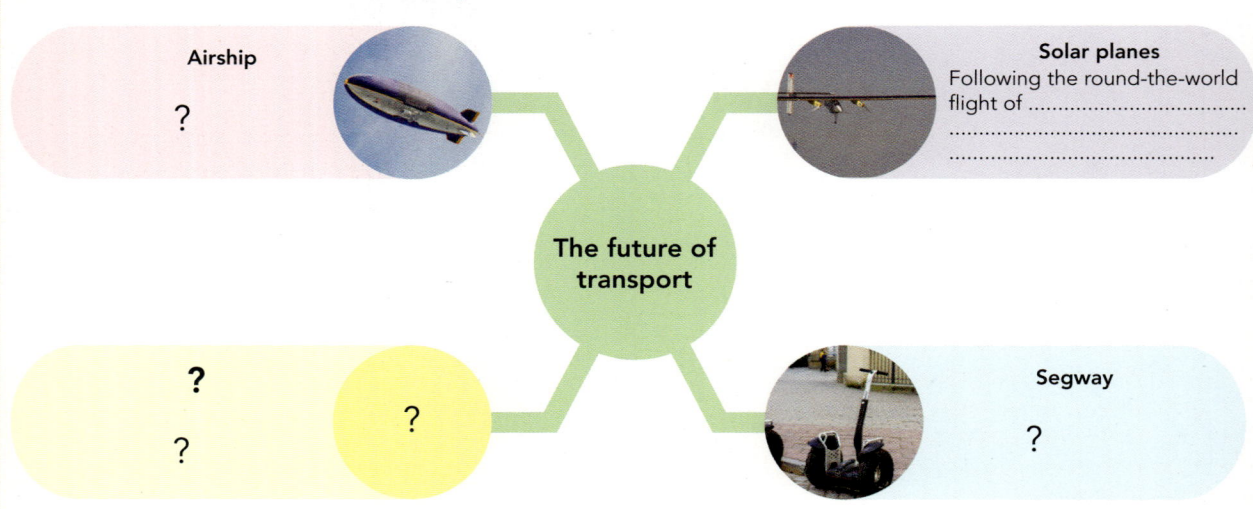

Airship
?

Solar planes
Following the round-the-world flight of ....
....
....

The future of transport

? ?

?

Segway
?

① **Make a list of all the types of transport you think there will be in the future.**
Here are some suggestions but there are others.

Airship   Drone   Electric bike
Maglev train
Segway   Solar plane   Jetpack
Flying car   SlideWalk
Driverless car

② **Divide into groups. Decide which form of transport each group will write about.**

③ **Work in groups.**
- Research your topic.
- Write a short text (about 50 words) about your topic.
- Find (or draw) a picture to illustrate your text.
- Present it clearly on paper.

My learning
What did you learn by doing this project?

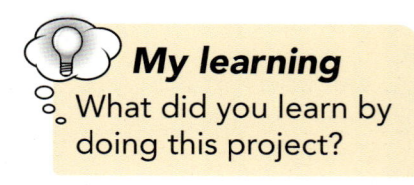

④ **Add your work to the class infographic.**

interact with peers; research and write a class infographic

Stories 8

Looking forward

This unit explores stories and storytelling.

You will read
- about what makes a great story
- three poems about stories, poems and words

You will listen
- to a traditional story

You will speak
- about favourite stories
- together to create a class or group story

You will write
- an exciting opening to a story
- a group story

You will learn
- some vocabulary to talk about stories and poems
- how to report questions
- about adjectives ending in *–ing* and *–ed*

Tell us a story

Listening: setting the scene

1 Look at these words. Find out the meaning of any words you don't know.

traveller   stone   soup   ingredients   cooking pot   villagers

2 Work in groups. All of the words above are used in a story. What do you think the story is about?

Listening: a story

1 🔊 Listen to part 1 and answer these questions.
  1. What did the traveller ask for?
  2. Why can't the villagers help him?
  3. What does the traveller start to make?
  4. What do you think will happen next?

2 Listen to part 2 and answer these questions.
  1. Which ingredients do the villagers find?
  2. What do they make together?
  3. What do you think will happen the next morning?

3 Listen to the end and answer these questions.
  1. What did the villagers want?
  2. What does the traveller tell them?
  3. Does the story have a happy ending?

4 Listen to the story again.

The traveller said to the villagers "… *it can teach you an important lesson*". What was the lesson?

Vocabulary: words in context

Match the underlined words to their meanings, on page 85.

> The traveller pulled a large black stone from his pocket and ¹ <u>dropped</u> it into the pot.
>
> He ² <u>smelled</u> the soup and said, "Stone soup is ³ <u>tasty</u> but it's always better with a few onions."
>
> The traveller ⁴ <u>stirred</u> the onions into the soup.
>
> Together they found all the ⁵ <u>ingredients</u> they needed for a ⁶ <u>thick</u> healthy soup.

84   *listen to extended narrative; implied meaning*

a   all the foods used in a dish
b   food that is nice to eat
c   let something fall
d   mix food by moving it around with a spoon
e   notice something by using your nose
f   when a soup is not moving easily: the opposite of *thin*

Use of English: reporting questions

1 Put these sentences in the correct order.

> a   He asked if anyone had an onion or two.
> b   The traveller asked the villagers if they wanted to share stone soup with him.
> c   The teacher asked the traveller if he would sell his magic stone.
> d   The traveller said the soup really needed some tomatoes. He asked if anyone could help.
> e   The traveller asked why they would give money for a stone?

2 Which words did the traveller use to ask the questions in sentences a–e above?

3 Look at sentences a–e above. Answer these questions about *yes / no questions*.

1   Which reporting verb is used in all the reported questions?
2   Is the word order the same in the questions and the reported questions?
3   What happens to the 'helping' verbs (*Do, Does*) when the questions are reported?
4   What happens to the question marks when the questions are reported?
5   Which new word is added to all the reported questions?
6   What happens to the verb tenses and pronouns?
7   What happens to verbs such as *can* and *will*?

4 Report these questions from the story.

"Do you have anything to eat?"   The traveller …

"Will you sit down and eat with me?"   The traveller …

5 Look at sentence e in activity **1** above. Answer these questions about *question-word* questions.

1   Do we use *if* in this kind of reported question?
2   Do we use the *question-word* in this kind of reported question?

6 Report these questions from the story.

"What type of soup are you making?"   The boy asked …

"Where will you go tomorrow?"   The villagers asked the traveller …

Language tip

There are two types of questions in English:

Yes / no questions have small 'helping' verbs (for example, *do, does, did, is, was, can, will*) before the subject of the sentence. They ask for the answer *yes* or *no*.

Question-word questions start with *who, what, where, when, how* or *why*.

deduce meaning of vocabulary; reported speech

Making great stories

Reading: setting the scene

1. Read this dictionary definition of *fiction*. What is *non-fiction*?

   fiction **uncountable noun** books and stories about people and events that are not real

2. Work in groups. Discuss these questions. Use a dictionary to find out the meaning of any words you don't know.
   - Do you prefer reading fiction or non-fiction?
   - Which types of fiction do you like to read?

     crime   romance   adventure   science fiction   humour   horror

   - What do you enjoy in a story?

     lots of action   a happy ending   lots of laughs
     interesting characters

Reading: exploring the text

1. Is the story *Stone Soup* fiction or non-fiction?

2. Look at the text below – DON'T read it yet.
   1. Do you think it is fiction or non-fiction?
   2. What features of the text can you see that help you to answer the question above?

3. Read the text to see if your answers to activity 2 are correct.

What makes a great story?

Which stories are the best ones you have read or heard? Now is the time to think about your experience of stories, and to use this experience to create your own story.

> All stories have five elements:
>
> - Characters
>   Think carefully about who is in your story. Your main character needs to be someone readers are interested in. They don't have to be perfect (nobody is!), but they must be someone the reader can care about.
>
>   Don't include too many characters in a short story.
>
> - Setting
>   This is where and when your story is set or takes place. For some stories, the setting isn't too important. However, for stories set a long time in the past or in the future, you will need to describe the setting carefully.

typical features of a story

- Plot
  This is the different events that make up the story. To make the plot interesting, your main character needs to face a problem or a challenge. He, she or it (in some stories the characters are animals) has to find a solution to the problem or to complete the challenge.

- Theme
  This is a main point that the story tries to tell or teach us. You don't have to shout out the theme. Let it grow out of what takes place in the story, so that the readers feel that they have learned it for themselves.

- Structure
  This is how the story is put together. All stories need to have a beginning, a middle and an end. But a story doesn't have to start at the beginning. To make things interesting, you can jump straight into the action (and this way you don't give the reader any time to get bored).

Reading: understanding the text

Match the elements of stories with their meanings.

1 characters
2 setting
3 plot
4 theme
5 structure

a how the story is made
b who is in the story
c what the story is about
d when and where the story takes place
e what happens in the story

Vocabulary: words in context

Find words in the text with the following meanings:

1 to make something new happen [look in the introduction to the text]
2 important parts of something [see introduction]
3 as good as possible [see **Characters**]
4 things that happen [see **Plot**]
5 something that is difficult to do [see **Plot**]
6 events that make part of the story [see **Structure**]

Speaking: using the text

Work in pairs. Copy and complete the table about the *Stone Soup* story.

Characters	
Setting	
Plot — beginning	
middle	
end	
Theme (or lesson)	

read for main points; interact with peers

Use of English: adjectives ending in –ing and –ed

1 Work in pairs. Follow the instructions.

1. We can make adjectives from verbs. Find two in the last sentence of the text on page 87.
2. Some of these adjectives end in –ing. Make a list of some you know.
3. Some of these adjectives end in –ed. Make a list of some you know.
4. Look at your lists. Which (–ing or –ed) describes a feeling? Which describes the cause of the feeling?

2 Copy and complete these sentences using an –ing or –ed adjective.

> I read a really ¹ _____ story last night. Nothing happened in it but my parents wanted me to read it. I was so ² _____ that I fell asleep.
> We were really ³ _____ by the ending of the film. We didn't expect it.
> It had a really clever and ⁴ _____ plot.

3 Copy and complete the table. Write lists of three things for each adjective.

Things I find …			Things that make me …		
frightening	amusing	amazing	annoyed	pleased	worried

4 Work in groups. Talk about the things in your lists.

> I find dark nights frightening.

> Really! I don't mind the dark, but I find horror films frightening!

Speaking: storytelling

1 Listen to your teacher and work together to make a class story.

2 Work in groups. Make a story using all of the words in one of the word roses.

mystery	detective	adventure
ancient camel	canoe criminal	perfect enemy
tasty pirate	helicopter parachute	festival vehicle
confusing	rock climbing	celebration

adjectives from participles; telling stories

3 Change groups. Tell your story.

4 Copy and complete this story plan about your story.

Characters	
Setting	
Plot beginning	
middle	
end	

Writing: starting a story

1 Read the *Skills tip* box. Then match the three story starters.

1	action	a	"It was here! I know it was here," cried Maria.
2	speech	b	Old Ropo's home was as dark, dirty and dangerous as he was.
3	description	c	Carl screamed as he flew out through the window into the dark night.

Skills tip
When you write a story, you need to have an exciting start to make your reader want to read on. There are three ways you can do this, by using:
- action
- speech
- description.

2 Write the opening paragraph of the story you made in the Speaking lesson.
- Make it interesting or exciting. You want the reader to read the rest of the story.
- Use action, speech or description for your first sentences. If one way doesn't work well, try another.

3 Work in pairs. Read your opening paragraphs to each other.

My learning
Think about the paragraph you have written and what your partner said when you read it out.

How could you make it better?

write a story with appropriate style and register

Focus on Literature

Three poems: story, poem, words

1 **Discuss.**
- What is the difference between a story and a poem?
- Read these dictionary definitions. Which one is which?

¹_____ **noun**
a piece of writing in which the words are chosen for their beauty and sound, and are written in short lines

²_____ **noun**
a description of some events (traditional, imaginary or true)

2 *Reading* on page 91 is a poem about stories. Read it and answer these questions.
1. Do you agree with what the poet says?
2. What do you notice about the last words in lines 2 and 4?

3 *Poetry* on page 91 is a poem about poetry. Read it and answer these questions.
1. Which lines rhyme?
2. What does the poet think about poetry?
   a. It has nothing to do with roses, the sky, flies or the sea.
   b. It is impossible to say what poetry is.
   c. It is not about the thing, but what the thing means to us.
3. Work in pairs. Write some more lines for this poem.
   Start: Not the sun, but …
              Not the story, but …

4 *I like words* on page 91 is a poem about words. Read it and answer these questions.
1. This poem has four verses. What do you notice about each verse?
2. Which lines in the verses rhyme?
3. Think of examples of:
   a. words you cannot spell   b. words of love that keep you warm
   c. words that make you glad   d. words that hurt
   e. words that make you sad.
4. Work in pairs. Write a new verse for this poem.
   Start: Words in stories.

Reading by Marchette Chute
A story is a special thing.
　　　The ones I have read,
They do not stay inside the book,
　　　They stay inside my head.

Poetry by Eleanor Farjeon
What is Poetry? Who knows?
Not the rose, but the scent of the rose;
Not the sky, but the light in the sky;
Not the fly, but the gleam of the fly;
Not the sea, but the sound of the sea;
Not myself, but what makes me
See, hear and feel something that prose
Cannot; and what it is, who knows?

rose – a type of flower
scent – smell
fly – a small flying insect
gleam – a light that shows for a short time
prose – normal written language, not poetry

I like words by Steve Turner
I like words.
Do you like words?
Words aren't hard to find:
Words on walls and words in books,
Words deep in your mind.

Words in jokes
That make you laugh,
Words that seem to smell
Words that end up inside out,
Words you cannot spell.

Words of love
That keep you warm,
Words that make you glad.
Words that hit you, words that hurt,
Words that make you sad.

I like words.
Do you like words?
Words come out and play.
Words are free and words are friends,
Words are great to say.

mind – brain
joke – something that you say to make people laugh

Project: The map

In this project you are going to work in groups to create, plan and write an adventure story called *The map*.

> Characters in adventure stories often go on exciting and dangerous journeys. They don't know what will happen on these difficult journeys. At the end, they overcome the dangers and there is usually a happy ending.

1 Discuss what part the map will play in your story.

- What is a map?
- What things are found on a map?
- Where might we find a map?
- Why might a map be important in a story?

2 Discuss the key elements of your story. Start with these suggestions:

- *Who?*   pirates, treasure hunters, spacemen, police, scientists
- *Where?*   ship, island, desert, forest, space, under the sea
- *When?*   long ago, late at night, in the future, in the school holidays
- *What?*   find map in a bottle / inside a book / on the internet
- *Why?*   map to rescue someone / to find treasure / to find a new planet

3 Plan your story. Copy and complete the plan.

Characters	
Setting	
Plot How to start the story Journey to where? Which dangers? How to overcome the dangers	

4 Write your story.

- Work together with your group. One of you can write as the others tell the story. Or each of you in the group can write a different part of the story.
- Start with an exciting opening paragraph.
- When you have finished writing your story, read it aloud and look for ways to make it better.

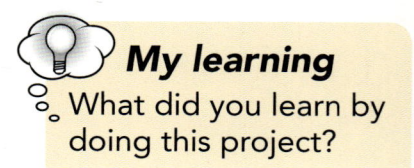

My learning
What did you learn by doing this project?

brainstorm; plan, draft, edit; compose a group story

Mid-year review

Reading: setting the scene

Look at the photo. Discuss.
- What is bungee jumping?
- Have you ever done a bungee jump? Do you know anyone who has?
- Would you like to do a bungee jump? Why / Why not?

Reading: exploring the text

1 Look at the text.
  1 Where do you find texts like this?
  2 What is the headline?
  3 What do you think it is about?

2 Read the article to check your answer.

Amazing escape in bungee accident

A young woman had a lucky escape when her bungee jump went badly wrong recently. She fell 111 metres from the Victoria Falls Bridge into the Zambezi River below.

Bungee jumping is an extreme sport in which people jump off high buildings or bridges. A cord should stop their fall but for Erin Langworthy, who is 22 and from Australia, this didn't happen. The cord broke and she found herself in the fast-moving water.

Happily, she swam to some rocks, which she then held on to. She was in the river for 40 minutes before she was rescued by staff from the bungee jump company. After a week in hospital, Erin has now returned home. She said that she hoped to do another bungee jump one day!

Reading: understanding the text

Put these events in the order they happened to Erin Langworthy.

| 1 be rescued | 2 get better in hospital | 3 go home |
| 4 hold on to rocks | 5 jump | 6 swim |

Use of English: language in context

Look in the text to find the following:
1. a relative clause. (Look back to page 54 for help.) Why is it used in this sentence?
2. a compound adjective. (See page 64.) What does the adjective describe?
3. a passive verb. (See page 32.) Who did the action?
4. a verb in the present perfect tense. (See page 43.) Why is this tense used and not the past simple?
5. an example of reported speech. (See page 34.) What were the words she said?

Vocabulary: words in context

1 Read these sentences about adventure sports. Choose the best word to complete them.

1. Skydivers jump from planes and _____ through the air before opening a parachute.
   - a swim
   - b drop
   - c dive
2. Adventure sports aim to give as much _____ as possible.
   - a excitement
   - b relaxation
   - c rest
3. Many extreme sports are done at high _____ .
   - a movement
   - b speed
   - c fast
4. Adventure sports are _____ activities.
   - a out
   - b outside
   - c outdoor

2 Read these sentences about transport. Choose the best word to complete them.

1. There are too many _____ driving too fast on that road.
   - a trains
   - b machines
   - c vehicles
2. Solar cars get their _____ from the Sun.
   - a power
   - b strength
   - c force
3. We need to put some _____ in the car before we go on the motorway.
   - a power
   - b fuel
   - c drink
4. Old cars and lorries _____ a lot of pollution.
   - a produce
   - b create
   - c make

mid-year review

Speaking: discussing opinions

1 Think. What's your opinion about the following topics?

- a lizards as pets
- b learning English
- c modern art
- d extreme sports
- e social networks
- f green cars

2 Work in groups. Listen to what others have to say and discuss your own opinions.

I think …	In my opinion, …	I believe …	It seems to me that …
I couldn't agree more!	Exactly! That's my view, too.		
I agree, but …	That's a good point, but …	Yes, but what about …	
I can't agree with you because …	I agree / disagree because …		

Use of English: correction competition

Work in pairs. Read these instructions.

- Read the sentences. Four are correct but four are incorrect.
- You get one mark for each incorrect sentence you can find.
- You get two marks for each incorrect sentence you can correct.
- The winner is the pair with the most points.

1. I heard a noise. Is there anyone there?
2. Peter has just going shopping.
3. I've lived in this city for I was born.
4. I haven't got much money left.
5. The art gallery, which is full of expensive works of art, had a terrible fire last night.
6. Snowboarders use their bodies to change direction while ski down mountains.
7. As we all want to cut down on pollution, we need to use more environmentally friendly cars.
8. I'm thinking to visit the City Museum tomorrow. Do you want to come with me?

mid-year review

Listening: conversations

Listen to the three dialogues. Read these questions and choose the best answers.

1 Where are they going now?

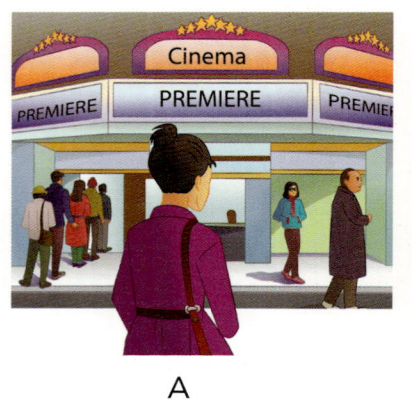

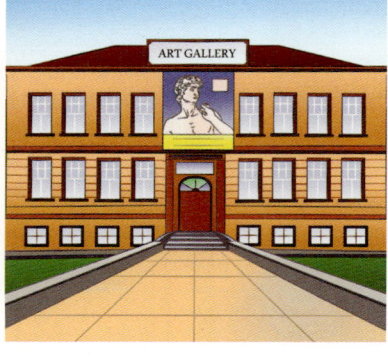

A   B   C

2 How will the family travel from home to their holiday?

A   B   C

3 Who is going on the holiday?

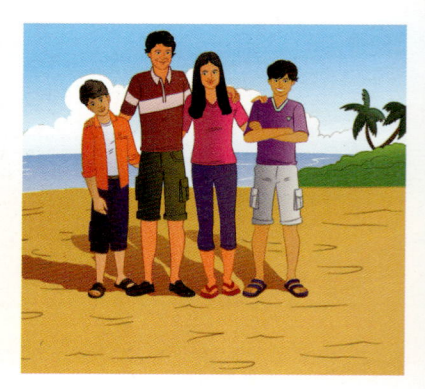

A   B   C

Use of English: rewording

For each question, copy and complete the second sentence so that it means the same as the first.

1. a Clothes in the mall are more expensive than those on the market.
   b Clothes in the mall aren't _____ as those in the market.
2. a The loud noise outside the window surprised us.
   b We _____ by the loud noise outside the window.
3. a Twenty computers were stolen from my father's office. They were all new.
   b Twenty computers, _____ all new, were stolen from my father's office.
4. a It's really boring to listen to the same music all the time.
   b I'm really _____ to the same music all the time.
5. a We won't be able to stay for long because the journey here was so slow.
   b _____ the journey here was so slow, we won't be able to stay for long.

Speaking: an interview

1 Work in groups.
- Think of a famous person you all know about. Share all the information you know.
- Choose one person in the group to play the role of your famous person.

2 Change groups.
- All the 'famous people' form one group. Prepare to answer questions from reporters.
- The rest of you play the role of reporters. Prepare questions to ask the famous people.

3 The reporters interview the famous people.

> Do you have any interesting stories to tell us?

> What are your plans for the future?

Writing: reporting an interview

Write a report about the interviews. Report some of the questions and answers.
Look at Workbook page 00 if you need help with reporting speech.

We asked if she had any interesting stories.

He said that he was going to America next month.

mid-year review

Speaking: what's happened?

1 Look at the photo. Read these questions and think of possible answers.

- Has she seen something?
- Has somebody said something?
- How does she feel now?
- What is she going to say?
- What will happen next?

2 Work in groups. Take turns to tell one another what you think has happened and what will happen next.

Writing: an email

1 Read this email. What does your cousin want to know about?

> Hi,
>
> How's my favourite cousin?
>
> I wanted to let you know I'm having a great time in England, and I'm learning a lot of English.
>
> How about you? You've been studying Grade 7 English for about half a year now. Are you getting on well? I'm sure you are. What have you learned so far? What have you enjoyed studying? Have you learned a lot of new English words? And what about the grammar? What have you found difficult? Maybe I can help you.
>
> What do you think you'll be doing for the rest of the year? I'll be back in three months – we can talk then.
>
> Al

2 Work in pairs. Discuss your answers to these questions about learning English this year.

- What have you learned?
- What have you enjoyed studying?
- What have you found difficult?
- What do you hope to do for the rest of the year?

3 Write an email to reply to your cousin.

mid-year review

Wildlife under threat

9

Looking forward

This unit explores some animals that are in danger, and what can be done to help them.

You will read
- about cheetahs and how they have been helped in one country
- about how to classify animals
- about endangered animals for a project

You will listen
- to a scientist talking about three endangered animals

You will speak
- about what can be done to help endangered animals
- in a role-play meeting about cheetahs

You will write
- using noun phrases to make your writing more interesting
- a report of a meeting

You will learn
- about modal verbs
- the conjunctions *so … that* and *such … that*
- *why* clauses

Endangered animals

Listening: setting the scene

1 You are going to listen to a talk about endangered animals.
- What does the word *danger* mean? Give examples of some dangers.
- What do you think *endangered* means? Which animals can you name that are endangered?

2 Read these animal fact files. Which information is missing?

Name: tiger
Key facts: largest of the cat family; weighs ^{1} _____ ; 3.3m long
Lives: ^{2} _____
Numbers: ^{3} _____ (2015)
Threats: losing land (now have ^{4} _____ of land they used to have); hunting for their skins
Good news: a recent small increase in numbers

Name: leatherback turtle
Key facts: has lived on Earth for more than ^{5} _____ years
Lives: oceans ^{6} _____
Numbers: unknown but falling quickly
Threats: ^{7} _____ (caught in nets); pollution (particularly ^{8} _____)
Good news: none

Name: mountain gorilla
Key facts: intelligent – can learn sign language
Lives: Central ^{9} _____
Numbers: ^{10} _____
Threats: war; losing forest; ^{11} _____ ; disease
Good news: 14% increase in numbers in the last ^{12} _____

Listening: a talk

1 🔊 Listen to the scientist talking. Which animal does he discuss first, second and last?

2 Listen again. Complete the fact files with the missing information.

Vocabulary: words in context

Match the words with their meanings.

> disease   hunt   increase   intelligent   land   net   ocean   skin

1 the outside layer of a person's or animal's body
2 a rise in the number or amount of something
3 to catch or kill an animal
4 a bag made of string or rope used to catch fish
5 a large area of salt water
6 an area of ground (used for farming or living on)
7 a serious illness
8 good at thinking, understanding and learning

listen for specific information

Speaking: what can we do about it?

1 Read the conversation. What are they talking about?

> The number of endangered animals is frightening. We <u>have to</u> do something about it!

> You're right, but what <u>should</u> we do?

> Well, we <u>could</u> stop throwing plastic bags away.

> That's a good idea. But we <u>must</u> do something to help the gorillas as well.

> Yes, but what <u>can</u> we do?

2 Look at the underlined words. They are all called modal verbs.

1. Which ones do we use to talk about something that is important to do?
2. Which one do we use to suggest something?
3. Which one do we use to talk about possibility?

> *Language tip*
> Modal verbs add meaning to main verbs.
>
> We don't use them to talk about facts. We use them to express ideas and opinions.
>
> *He is a hunter.* [fact]
> *He shouldn't be a hunter.* [opinion]

3 What do you think we can do to help endangered animals?

- Discuss in a group.
- Tell the class your ideas.

Use of English: modals

Work in pairs. Follow the instructions to play *modal noughts and crosses*.

- Write your name on five small pieces of paper.
- Take turns to choose a square in the table below. Make a sentence using the modal in the square.
    - If you both agree that your sentence is correct, put your paper on the square.
    - If you don't agree that a sentence is correct, ask your teacher to decide.
- The winner is the first one to get three papers in a straight line (top to bottom, side to side, or corner to corner).

shouldn't	have to	must
need to	mustn't	might not
could	should	ought to

can	might	couldn't
may not	didn't need to	shall
will have to	wouldn't	may

modal verbs 101

Helping the cheetah

Reading: setting the scene

Look at the photo below and discuss.
- What do you know about cheetahs?
- What do you think is the main threat to cheetahs?

Reading: exploring the text

1 Read the text quickly to answer these questions.
1. In 1925, how many cheetahs were there?
2. How many are there now?
3. Who killed 10 000 cheetahs in the 1980s?
4. What do the letters CCF mean?
5. In which country does the CCF work?

2 Read the headline and then read the text more slowly. What is the good news?

Study tip
When you read to find information, it is not always necessary to read every word. If you want to find a number, a date or a name, run your eyes over the text to look for numbers or capital letters.

Good news for one endangered big cat

The amazing cheetah is the fastest animal on land in the world. It can run at up to 120 kph. But the cheetah's speed does not protect it. In 1925 there were 100 000 cheetahs in Africa and Asia. Now there are probably fewer than 10 000.

The big problem for cheetahs is that they live too near to people. Often they live on, or close to, farms. Sometimes they hunt farm animals. To protect their animals, farmers shoot the cheetahs. In Namibia, where there is the largest number of cheetahs in the world, farmers killed 10 000 cheetahs during the 1980s.

In 1994 the Cheetah Conservation Fund (CCF) found a clever way to save the cheetahs. They gave dogs to farmers in Namibia. These dogs grow up with the sheep and goats, so they think of them as their family. If a cheetah comes near these animals, the dogs will protect them. Cheetahs do not like to fight, so will usually run away.

The result – the number of farm animals killed by cheetahs has fallen by over 90%. The farmers are happy and don't need to kill the cheetahs. The cheetahs lose a few meals but they are in less danger.

The CCF's programme has been so successful that it is now used in other countries.

read for specific information (scanning)

Reading: understanding the text

Copy and complete this fact file.

Name: cheetah
Key facts:
Lives:
Numbers:
Threats:
Good news:

Vocabulary: words in context

Find words in the text to match these meanings.

1 how fast something moves (paragraph 1)
2 to keep someone or something safe (paragraphs 1, 2 and 3)
3 to hurt or kill a person or animal by using a gun (paragraph 2)
4 something that is caused by something else (paragraph 4)
5 a plan of things to do (last paragraph)
6 in getting what you wanted (last paragraph)

Writing: using noun phrases

> *Language tip*
> A group of words that work together in a sentence to act like a noun is called a *noun phrase*. They can add interest and information to sentences.

1 Look at these sentences and answer the questions.

   a The cheetah   is   an animal.
   b The amazing cheetah   is   a fast animal.
   c The amazing cheetah   is   the fastest animal on land in the world.

   1 Which one is a simple sentence? It has nouns and a verb but doesn't tell us a lot of information.
   2 Which one has some adjectives to give more information and interest?
   3 Which one tells us the most? This is a complex sentence with noun phrases.

2 Use adjectives to make this sentence more interesting.

   • The _____ mountain gorilla is _____ animal.

   Now add more information.

   • The _____ mountain gorilla is _____ animal which _____

3 Work in pairs. Make complex sentences about the tiger and the leatherback turtle.

read for detail; deduce meaning of vocabulary; noun phrases

Use of English: conjunctions *so … that* and *such … that*

1 Look at the last sentence of the text on page 102. We could write it in two sentences.

The programme has been very successful. It is now used in other countries.

1 Which two words have been used to join the two sentences into one?
2 Which word is between them? Is it an adjective or a noun?

> **Language tip**
> A word, or words, that join two ideas in one sentence is called a *conjunction*. Some common conjunctions are *and, or, but*. Which others do you know?

2 Look at this sentence. It is similar but not the same.

The programme has been such a success that it is now used in other countries.

1 Does the sentence mean the same as the last sentence in the text?
2 Which two words does this sentence use to join the two parts?
3 Is *success* an adjective or a noun?

3 Complete these rules.

1 We use *so … that* with an _____ or adverb.
2 We use *such … that* with a _____.
3 They have the _____ meaning. They give a reason or explanation.

4 Complete these sentences using your own words.

- Cheetahs in Namibia were in such danger that …
- The CCF programme is so clever that …
- The dogs and the farm animals are such good friends that …
- The dogs are so big and strong that the cheetahs …

Speaking: role play

Work in groups of four. You are going to have a meeting about hunting cheetahs.

- Choose your roles. You all live in a country (not Namibia) that has wild cheetahs.
  You are:
  – a farmer   – a wildlife protection officer   – a local leader   – a tourism officer
- Read your role card and prepare what you want to say.
- Hold a meeting.
  – Introduce yourselves and say what you think.
  – Discuss the problem. Work together to try to find a solution.

The reasons why

Use of English: *why* clauses

1 Read what the four people said after the meeting. Match the people to what they say.

farmer   wildlife protection officer   local leader   tourism officer

a "The reason why I want to try the CCF programme here is that it is the best way to protect these endangered animals."
b "I want to see more tourists. That's why I support the CCF programme."
c "The reason why I will try the CCF programme is that I want to protect my animals from cheetahs."
d "I want to keep cheetahs away from our villages. That's why I don't support the new programme."

2 Copy and complete the sentences to give your own reasons.
- I like animals. That's why …
- The reason why we need to protect endangered animals is that …

Writing: a report

Write a short report about your meeting about the cheetahs.

1 Give your report a heading.

   Report of a meeting on [date] about the cheetah problem.

2 Introduce who you are and what you think about cheetahs.

   I am a …   My job is to …   The cheetahs …

3 Introduce the CCF programme.

   There is a programme to …   The CCF will …   The dogs will …   The farmers …

4 Give your opinions about the programme. Give reasons for your opinions.

   The reason why I (don't) support the CCF programme is that …

5 Say what you want to happen next.

   Now we should …   I think we must …
   We don't have to …

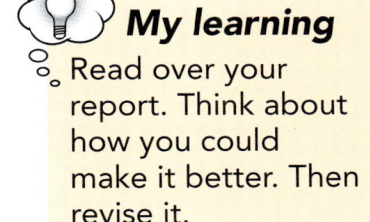

My learning
Read over your report. Think about how you could make it better. Then revise it.

relative clauses; use appropriate style, register and layout; develop coherent arguments

Focus on Science (Biology)

Scientists believe that there are between 5 and 15 million species of plants, animals and other living things in the world today. Of these, only about 1.5 million have been described and named. This includes about 300 000 types of plants, between 4 and 8 million species of insects, about 10 000 birds and 4000 mammals.

Because there are so many species, it helps to be able to classify them. That means, to put things into different groups to show how they are alike. If we look only at animals we can classify them into two main types: *vertebrates* and *invertebrates*.

- A vertebrate is an animal with a backbone. People are vertebrates. You can feel your own backbone if you put your hand on the middle of your back.
- Invertebrates don't have backbones. All insects are invertebrates.

Vertebrates are classified into five separate groups: *mammals*, *birds*, *fish*, *amphibians* and *reptiles*.

Mammals give birth to live babies.
They feed their babies with milk.
They use lungs to breathe.
They are warm-blooded.

Birds have feathers.
They have beaks.
They lay eggs.
They are warm-blooded.

Fish live in water.
They have fins.
They use gills to breathe.
They are cold-blooded.

Amphibians can live in water and on land.
They lay eggs in water.
They use lungs to breathe.
They are cold-blooded.

Reptiles have scales on their skin.
They lay eggs.
They use lungs to breathe.
They are cold-blooded.

A 
B 
C 
D 
E

1 Match the descriptions and the pictures.

2 These words are parts of animal bodies.
   a Match the words to the meanings.
   1 beak
   2 feather
   3 fin
   4 gill
   5 lungs
   6 scale

   a a small, hard flat part that covers a fish or reptile
   b a small part behind a fish's head, which it uses to breathe
   c a small tube with thin soft hairs that cover a bird
   d bags inside the body that fill with air for breathing
   e the hard part of a bird's mouth
   f the thin, flat part that comes out of a fish's body to help it swim

3 Find five of the animal body parts listed in activity 2 in the pictures on page 106. Which animal body part is not shown in the pictures?

4 Copy and complete the sentences with compound adjectives from the text.
   1 Mammals and birds have warm blood. We say they are _____
   2 Other types of animals are all _____.

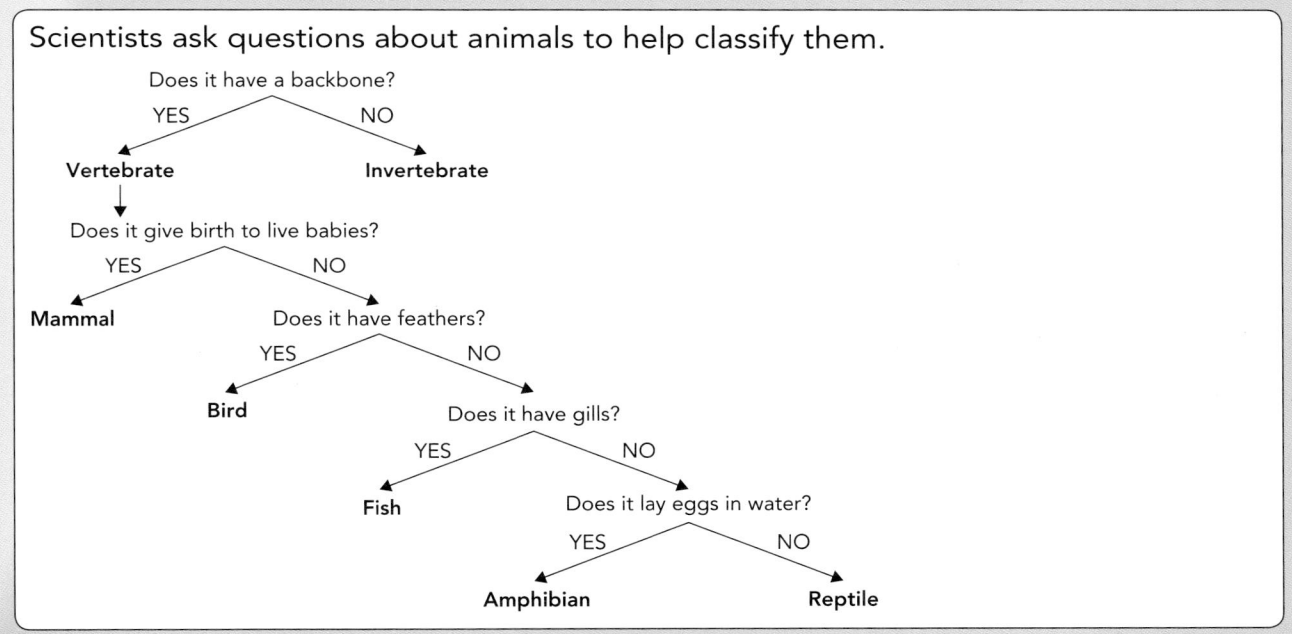

Scientists ask questions about animals to help classify them.

Does it have a backbone?
- YES → Vertebrate
- NO → Invertebrate

Does it give birth to live babies?
- YES → Mammal
- NO → Does it have feathers?
  - YES → Bird
  - NO → Does it have gills?
    - YES → Fish
    - NO → Does it lay eggs in water?
      - YES → Amphibian
      - NO → Reptile

---

5 Imagine you are a scientist and you have found these animals. Ask questions to classify them.
   1 It has a backbone. It doesn't have feathers or gills. It has a wet skin and can live on land or in water. It lays its eggs in water. What is it?
   2 It has a backbone and is warm-blooded. It doesn't have a beak, feathers, gills or fins. It doesn't lay eggs but it gives birth to live babies. What is it?
   3 It has a backbone. It has scales but it doesn't have feathers or gills. It is cold-blooded but it has lungs. It lays eggs but it doesn't lay them in water. What is it?

Project: endangered animals

In this project you are going to work together to research an endangered animal and to decide what can be done to help it. You will then tell the class what you have learned about the animal.

orangutan   polar bear   monarch butterfly   rhino

1. Work in groups. Decide on an endangered animal to learn about. It can be one of the animals in the pictures above, or you can search online for other endangered animals.

2. Do some research to find out about your animal. You need to know the following:
   - some key facts or interesting information
   - where it lives
   - how many there are now (and maybe how many there used to be)
   - the threats it faces (and why it is endangered)
   - what can be done to help it.

   Also search for a picture of the animal to show to the class.

3. Prepare your presentation. Decide how you want to organise your information. You could:
   - make a fact file like the ones on page 100
   - make a poster
   - show a picture and give a talk like the one you listened to at the beginning of this unit.

4. Tell the class about your animal. Try to make everyone interested and want to help your animal. Be ready to answer questions.

5. Listen to the presentations of other groups. Write notes about:
   - which animal it is and key facts about it
   - the threats the animal faces
   - what can be done to help.

   My learning
   What did you learn by doing this project?

   Ask questions if there is something you don't understand.

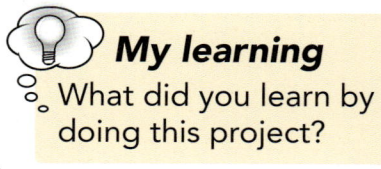

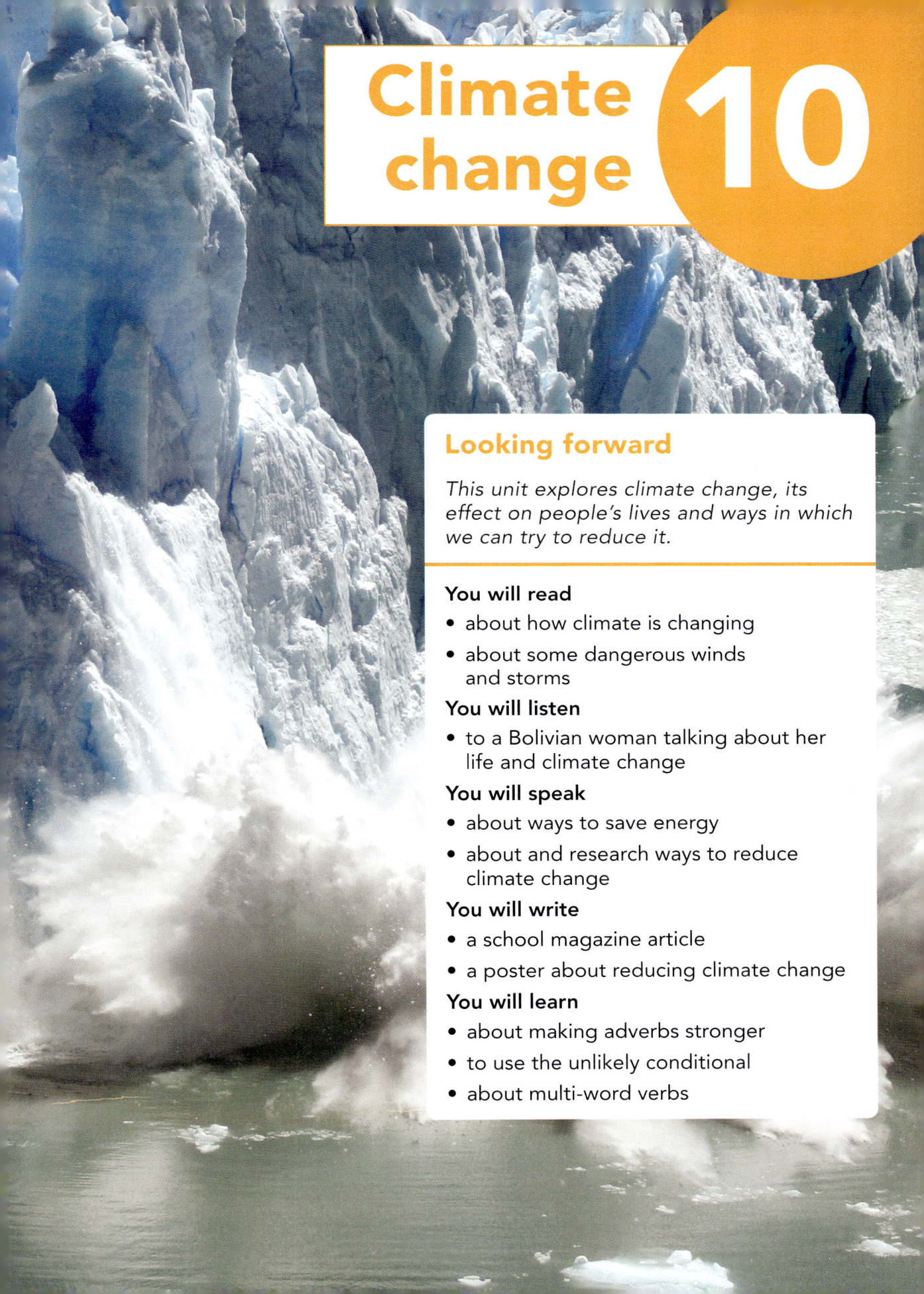

Climate change 10

Looking forward

This unit explores climate change, its effect on people's lives and ways in which we can try to reduce it.

You will read
- about how climate is changing
- about some dangerous winds and storms

You will listen
- to a Bolivian woman talking about her life and climate change

You will speak
- about ways to save energy
- about and research ways to reduce climate change

You will write
- a school magazine article
- a poster about reducing climate change

You will learn
- about making adverbs stronger
- to use the unlikely conditional
- about multi-word verbs

Does it matter?

Reading: setting the scene

Discuss.

- Explain the meaning of these words. Use a dictionary, if necessary.

  Earth   North Pole   South Pole   glacier   melt

- What do *climate change* and *global warming* mean?
- What do you know about climate change?

Reading: exploring the text

1. Look at the graph in the text. What does it show?
2. Read the title. What do you think the text will be about?
3. Read the text to find out if you were correct.

So what if Earth gets a tiny bit warmer?

The sky is still blue. Trees are still green. Wind still blows. Clouds are still white and lovely. Rain still pours from the sky. Snow falls, and it still gets really cold sometimes in some places. Earth is still beautiful.

So, what is the problem? What is the issue with climate change and global warming?

Well, after careful research and study, scientists have seen some very worrying changes. These changes are happening fast – much faster than changes have happened before in Earth's long history.

Air temperatures have increased by around 0.5 °C during the past century. Since the start of the twenty-first century, almost every year has been the warmest on record. In the past 50 years, Earth has warmed twice as fast as in the 50 years before that. Average temperatures around the world are now more than 1 °C warmer than they were in 1880.

Between 1900 and 2000 the sea level rose by 17 cm. In the past ten years, the sea level has risen much more quickly. By 2099 the sea level may be 0.5 metres higher than in 2000. If the ice and snow at the North and South Poles and in the glaciers melts even more quickly, the sea level could be higher than this.

It may seem that these changes aren't much. However, we are talking here about averages, and across the whole Earth. This means that there could be a lot of changes in the future.

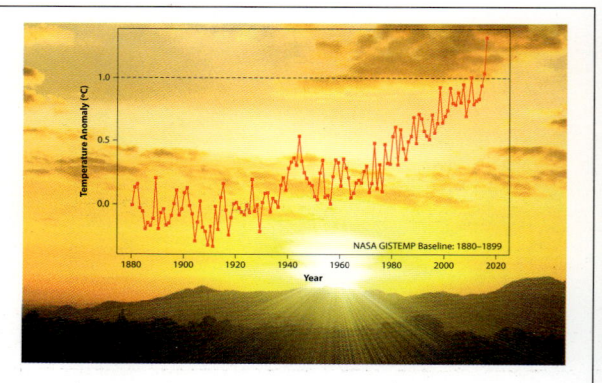

Reading: understanding the text

1 Look at the structure of the text and answer these questions.
1. How many paragraphs does it have?
2. Which paragraph introduces the problem?
3. Which paragraphs give evidence about the problem?
4. Which paragraph points to the result of this problem?
5. What do the other two paragraphs do?
6. Which paragraph does the graph support?

2 Are scientists more worried about changes to the climate or about how quickly these changes are happening?

3 Does the text tell us about climate change or about the results of climate change?

Vocabulary: words in context

1 Look at paragraph 1.
1. Find a verb that describes the movement of wind.
2. Find a verb that describes how rain falls.

2 Find these words in the text and match them to their meanings.

1	tiny	a	an important subject (that people talk about)
2	issue	b	to go up
3	rise (rose, risen)	c	to look like
4	seem	d	the result you get when you add two or more amounts together and divide the total by the number of amounts you added together
5	average	e	very small

Use of English: making adverbs stronger and weaker

Discuss.
1. The third paragraph tells us that recently changes to the climate have been happening *fast*. Are they happening *faster*, *a bit faster*, *a lot faster*, *much faster* or *very much faster* than before?
2. We can add words to make adverbs stronger when we compare. Find other examples in the text that make *fast* or *quickly* stronger.
3. Think of other examples that can make adverbs stronger. Use them in sentences.
4. We can use *not as …*, *less*, *much less* and *far less* with adverbs to make them less strong, or weaker, when we compare. Think of more examples and use them in sentences.

> In some years the air temperature increases less quickly than in other years.

recognise text features; understand detail of an argument; comparative degree adverb structures

A changing world

Listening: setting the scene

1 Work in pairs. Discuss the question.

If the climate changes, how will it change the life of people?

2 You are going to listen to Lucia from Bolivia talking about her life near to the mountain of Illimani. Look on a map to find Bolivia and Illimani.

Listening: a woman talks about her life

1 🔊 Read the questions. Then listen and answer.

1 How has the climate changed in Bolivia?
2 What job does Lucia do?
3 Does she have a family?
4 Is Lucia happy? Why / Why not?

2 Lucia explains how climate change may make her family leave their home. Match the sentences to complete Lucia's explanation.

1 As the climate gets warmer,
2 If the glaciers melt,
3 If there was no snow on Illimani,
4 If there was no water,
5 If the crops didn't grow,
6 If they had nothing to eat,

a the crops wouldn't grow.
b the glaciers melt.
c the people would have nothing to eat.
d the people would need to leave the village.
e there will be less snow and ice on the mountain.
f there would be no water coming down the mountain.

3 At the end, Lucia talks about a disease (a bad illness). What is the disease called? What do you know about it?

Vocabulary: words in context

1 Listen again. Copy and complete the sentences.

1 Without this water, farmers cannot grow _____.
2 The snow and ice are _____ day-by-day, year-by-year.
3 Everything _____ water.

2 Match the missing words above with these meanings.

a going away
b needs
c plants that people grow for food

112 *listen for main points and specific information; recognise opinion*

Use of English: the unlikely conditional

1 Look at the six sentences you completed in Listening: a woman talks about her life.

1 Which sentence talks about things that are happening now, and so is a fact?
2 Which sentence talks about things that are possible and likely to happen?
3 Which sentences talk about things that are possible but less likely to happen?

> *Language tip*
> Conditionals are sentences with two parts (both parts have a verb). One part often starts with *if* (but sometimes it starts with *unless* or *when*). The other part says what happens as a result of the *if* part. There are different types of conditional sentences, each using different verb tenses.

2 Look at the structures of the three types of sentences.

1 Which type has present simple tense verbs in both parts of the sentence?
2 Which type has a present simple tense in the first part of the sentences, and *will* + verb in the second part?
3 Which type has a past simple tense in the first part of the sentence, and *would* + verb in the second part?

3 It's not very likely, but imagine that you were made President of Earth. What would you do to stop climate change?

> If I was President of Earth, I'd …

4 What would happen? Play a game.

Work in groups. One person says a sentence. The next person makes a sentence using the second part of the previous sentence and adding their own idea.

> If I had lots of money, I'd buy my family a new house.

> If I bought my family a new house, we'd have a swimming pool and a helicopter.

> If we had a helicopter, …

5 Compare these two sentences.

- If the crops did not grow, the people would have nothing to eat.
- Unless the crops grew, the people would have nothing to eat.

1 Do they have the same meaning?
2 *Unless* in the second sentence has the same meaning as which two words in the first sentence?

6 Work in pairs. Change these sentence to use *unless*.

1 If it wasn't cold, it wouldn't snow on the mountain.
2 If it didn't snow, there would be no water coming down the mountain.
3 If there was no water coming down the mountain, the crops wouldn't grow.

second conditional clauses 113

What can we do?

Speaking: saving energy

1 Work in groups. Read and then discuss.

> **What can we do to stop or reduce global warming?**
>
> To answer this question we have to understand what causes it. When we burn or use fuels such as oil, petrol, coal and gas to make energy, they produce carbon dioxide (CO_2). The carbon dioxide stays in the air and stops heat from escaping out to space. So, the more carbon dioxide there is in the air, the warmer Earth will get.
>
> Therefore, to slow down global warming, we need to reduce the amount of carbon dioxide we produce on Earth. One way is to use less energy. Here are ten ways we can save energy:
>
> - Turn off lights when we leave a room.
> - Turn off TVs and computers when we are not using them.
> - Don't leave TVs on standby – they still use energy.
> - Turn off mobile phone and laptop chargers when we are not using them.
> - Don't boil a lot of water for a drink if we only need a little.
> - Have short showers to save hot water.
> - Walk or use a bike for short journeys rather than a car.
> - Use a bus or train for longer journeys rather than a car.
> - When it's cold, wear more clothes. Turn down the heating.
> - When it's hot, wear thin clothes. Turn down the cooling.

- Which of these ten ways to save energy do you *always* do? Are there others that you do *sometimes*?
- Which other ways can you think of to use less energy?
- Make a list of the five most important ways to save energy, in order of importance. Use the list above and your own ideas.

2 Present your group's list to the class. Discuss with other groups.

> Oh, really! I'm surprised – we think … is more important.

> Do you really think that's important? Why?

interact with peers to give opinions; respond and link comments

Vocabulary: multi-word verbs

1 Read these sentences from the text and answer the questions.

- <u>Turn off</u> the lights when you leave the room.
- <u>Turn down</u> the heating.
1. What is the opposite of *turn off*?
2. What is the opposite of *turn down*?

2 *Turn off*, *turn on*, *turn down* and *turn up* are all multi-word verbs. Do you know any others with the verb *turn*?

3 Work in pairs. Make sentences with the multi-word verbs in the box. Use a dictionary, if necessary.

turn into	turn out	turn over	turn to

Writing: a magazine article

1 Imagine that you have been asked to write an article for the school magazine. The title of the article is *Five top ways to save energy*.

- Decide which five ways you want to write about.
- Write a short introduction for your article. Explain why the topic is important, and why everyone should help to save energy.
- Present your five ways to save energy. Give a supporting reason for each one:
    1. Turn off the lights when you leave a room. This not only saves energy, but it also saves money, so it will make your parents happy!
- Write a short conclusion. Try to persuade your readers to do what you have suggested.

2 Work in pairs. Check and correct your articles.

- **Punctuation** Have you used capital letters at the start of each sentence and full stops (or question marks) at the end? Have you used commas?
- **Spelling** Are there any words you are not sure how to spell? Use a dictionary, if necessary.
- **Layout** Have you used paragraphs or clear sections, with numbers for each of the five ways?
- **What it says** Are the five ways made clear? Does each one have a supporting reason or example?

Did you know…?
Before a book or article is *published*, it is always checked (or *edited*) by an *editor*. The editor will make corrections and make suggestions about how the *work* can be made better. The *author* then rewrites the work.

3 Rewrite your article so that it is ready to be published in the school magazine.

prepositional and phrasal verbs; develop coherent arguments; edit

Focus on the World

Winds of the world

Hurricanes, typhoons and cyclones

These huge storms start in areas just to the north or south of the Equator. Near to North and Central America these storms are called *hurricanes.* In the east of the Pacific they are called *typhoons,* and in the Indian Ocean and near to Australia they are called *cyclones.*

All the storms start above warm seas of 30°C or more. Once the storms are very large, they begin to spin around. At the centre of the storm, there is always an *eye* where there are only light winds. But around this eye, winds can blow at up to 300 kilometres an hour.

When these storms move from the sea to land, they bring heavy rain, very strong winds and big waves. They can cause serious problems. In 1970 the Bhola cyclone killed 300 000 people in Bangladesh. More recently, Hurricane Katrina killed 1800 people and flooded 80% of the city of New Orleans in the state of Louisiana in the USA.

A hurricane over Central America, showing the eye and the winds spinning around it

Tornadoes

A tornado is a tall, thin column of air which comes down from a thunderstorm to the ground. It spins around very fast, up to 450 kilometres an hour, but moves quite slowly across the land. As the tornado spins, it pulls rocks, trees, cars and even houses up into the air and then drops them somewhere else.

It is not really understood how tornadoes begin, grow and disappear. However, we do know that they can start when warm, wet winds meet cool, dry winds. Air starts to rise up and then begins to spin.

Tornadoes can happen anywhere in the world, but most tornadoes, and the most dangerous ones, can be seen in North America. The USA has about 1200 tornadoes each year. Canada, which has the second most tornadoes, has fewer than 100 a year.

Monsoons

Monsoons are simpler to understand. They always blow from a cold area to a warm area, usually from a cool sea onto hot land. They usually happen at the same time every year.

Most monsoons bring rain to the land. This rain is very important; for example, most of the rain in India comes from monsoons. If a monsoon doesn't happen in any year, it can be very serious because the land will stay dry and crops won't grow. However, the monsoon rains can be very heavy and they can flood the land. The 2005 monsoon in India killed more than a thousand people.

read non-fiction text

1   Match these names from the text to the places on the map.

Australia   Canada   Central America   Equator   India
Indian Ocean   North America   Pacific Ocean   USA

2   Answer these questions.

1 What is the difference between a hurricane, a typhoon and a cyclone?
2 Which of the winds blow the fastest?
   a hurricanes / typhoons / cyclones   b tornadoes   c monsoons
3 Which of the winds don't spin around?
   a hurricanes / typhoons / cyclones   b tornadoes   c monsoons
4 Which of the winds are most dangerous?
   a hurricanes / typhoons / cyclones   b tornadoes   c monsoons
5 Which of the winds brings the most good for people?
   a hurricanes / typhoons / cyclones   b tornadoes   c monsoons

3   Match these words from the text to their meanings.

1 spin   a a line of water on the top of the sea
2 wave   b cover a place with water
3 serious   c the top part of the land where people walk
4 flood   d turn around and around quickly
5 ground   e very bad, and making people worried or afraid

read non-fiction text; understand main points

Project: reducing climate change

In this project you are going to make a poster about one way to help reduce climate change. You will then give a talk to the class about it.

1 Work in groups. Choose one of these ways that can help to reduce climate change:

- reduce (use fewer things, so that we don't need to use energy to produce so many new things)
- reuse (use things more than once, so that we don't need to buy so much)
- recycle (send things to be made into something new, so that we don't throw so much away)
- save energy on transport (using green cars and other environmentally friendly transport)
- save energy at home (for example, by using things that use less energy, turning things off)
- save energy in other buildings (for example, schools, shops, offices)
- buy food grown locally (so that it is not transported from other countries, which wastes energy)
- use other types of energy that don't produce CO_2 (for example, solar energy, wind power)
- plant trees (trees use CO_2 and reduce the amount of it in the air)
- anything else you can think of!

2 Find out as much as you can about your topic. You will find a lot of information online, but you will also find information at your school.

3 Plan a poster about your topic. A good poster should be clear and interesting.

- Choose a few key points. Don't include too much information.
- Give it a title. This should be short and written in large letters for everyone to see.
- You don't have to use full sentences. You can use notes, with numbers and bullet points.
- Write clearly, with words large enough to be read from a distance.
- Make it look good. Include pictures or diagrams, and use colour.

4 Work together as a group to make your poster.

5 Prepare your talk. Make sure that everyone in the group has a chance to speak, and that the poster is used.

6 Look at the other posters and listen to the talks. Think of questions to ask. Which is the best poster?

> **My learning**
> What did you learn by doing this project?

interact with peers to negotiate a task; use subject-specific vocabulary

Review 4

> *Study tip*
> It's review time again!

Speaking: looking back

Look back through Units 9 and 10.

1 Find one photo you like. Say why you like it.
2 Which activity did you enjoy the most? Say why you liked it and what you learned from doing it.

Reading: a quiz

1 Work in pairs. Find the answers to these questions in Units 9 and 10.

1 Where do mountain gorillas live?
2 How fast can a cheetah run?
3 How many species of birds have been named by scientists?
4 By how much did the sea rise between 1900 and 2000?
5 What do we call the place that is the furthest point north on Earth?

2 Write five more questions to ask about Units 9 and 10.

3 Work with another pair. Ask and answer your questions.

Writing: an email

Imagine that the students in your school have given money to support endangered animals. Your school now wants students to decide which *one* animal the money will support.

Write an email to give your opinion.

- Say which animal you want to help.
- Give some information about the animal.
- Give reasons why you think the money should support the animal.

Vocabulary: what are these words?

1 a large sea (for example, the Pacific)
2 to get bigger in some way (the opposite of *decrease*)
3 a type of animal that is warm-blooded, has lungs, gives birth to live babies and feeds them with milk
4 to prepare and make copies of newspapers, magazines or books, ready to read
5 the part of the sea which surfers ride on with their boards

Listening: what's missing?

1 This is what Lucia from Bolivia said. Think about how to fill the gaps 1–7.

"I have two daughters and one son who were born here in the village. I'm very worried when I see Illimani losing its snow and ice. The snow and ice [1] _____ day by day, year by year. The sun is stronger. It doesn't snow as much. We're very worried."

"Everything ² _____ water. I have some land where I grow potatoes, beans and other vegetables. If there is water, we ³ _____ crops; if not, we can't."

"In 30 or 40 years' time, or maybe a bit more, there ⁴ _____ no snow and ice left on Illimani. For my children that would be terrible. If there was no snow, there ⁵ _____ no water coming down. If there was no water, my children ⁶ _____ Where would they go?"

"The warmer climate also means there are more diseases, like malaria. Before there was no malaria in the mountains, but now people ⁷ _____ it there."

2 Now listen and write down the missing words.

Use of English: the unlikely conditional

1 Work in groups. Think of different ways to complete these sentences.

> If I went to live in another country, …

> If I could have any super power, …

> If I saw a tornado, …

2 Write down the best ending for each sentence.

Use of English: modals

1 Look at page 101. Make a noughts and crosses table.

2 Fill in your table with nine modal verbs from the box.

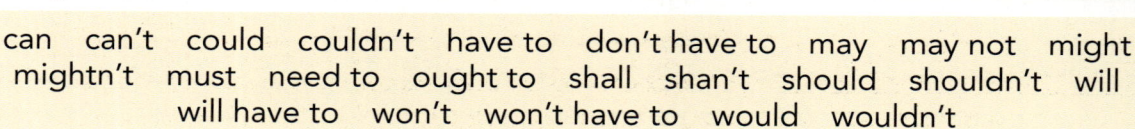

> can   can't   could   couldn't   have to   don't have to   may   may not   might   mightn't   must   need to   ought to   shall   shan't   should   shouldn't   will   will have to   won't   won't have to   would   wouldn't

3 Play *modal noughts and crosses*. You can find the rules on page 101.

Use of English: *so … that, such … that*

Work in pairs. Discuss.
- What would you do to prepare for a hurricane coming? What are the dangers?
- Think of ways to complete these sentences.

> Hurricanes can be so bad that …

> Hurricanes can be such a danger that …

Healthy living 11

Looking forward

This unit explores food, exercise and ways to have a healthy life.

You will read
- what some young people think about food and exercise
- some advice about healthy living
- about how food keeps you healthy

You will listen
- to someone talking about diets

You will speak
- about your experiences with food and diets
- about how you think people should keep healthy

You will write
- about how healthy you are
- a diary about your daily food, drink and exercise
- a questionnaire about healthy living

You will learn
- some words used to talk about healthy living
- to use the present perfect with *ever* and *never* to talk about experience
- to use some sentence adverbs
- to use the *–ing* form as a noun

Do diets work?

Listening: setting the scene

Discuss.

- Do you worry about how much you weigh?
- Have you ever been on a special diet to lose weight? Did it work?
- Does anyone in your family often go on diets? Do the diets work?

Listening: a lecture

You are going to listen to a health expert talking about diets.

1 Listen to the whole talk. Which of these topics does she talk about?

a how many diets there are
b which diets are the best
c why diets don't work
d the danger of diets
e healthy eating

2 Listen again. Are these sentences true or false?

1 There are many diets and people keep coming up with more.
2 Some people can make $300 billion a year from the diet business.
3 About half of the people who lose weight on a diet put it on again.
4 Diets don't work because our brains want us to keep fat for the future.
5 Some people who make and sell diets are not health or food experts.

3 Listen carefully once more. Think about what the speaker says.

1 Why does she think people come up with new diets?
2 What does she think about internet health bloggers?
3 What advice do you think she would give about going on a diet?
4 She says having too much fat for too long is not good for us. What do you think is her answer to losing weight without going on a special diet?

listen for the main points, specific information opinion and implied meaning

Vocabulary: words in context

1 Answer these questions about words from the lecture you listened to.
1. Some words have more than one meaning. You know the meaning of the adjective *fat* (for example, *a fat penguin*). What does *fat* mean when it is a noun (as in the lecture)?
2. The lecturer says that it isn't healthy to stop eating some kinds of food *because it means we don't get some of the nutrients that we need*. What do you think *nutrients* are?
3. Read this sentence from the lecture. What does it mean?
   Most of these bloggers have no training or experience in medicine or healthcare.
   a The people who write the blogs do not use medicine or follow their own diets.
   b The people who write the blogs are not doctors, nurses or anyone else who understands health.
   c The people who write the blogs do not use trains or medicine, or think about health.

2 Look at these sentences about people and their weight. Copy and complete the sentences with the opposite of the underlined words.
1. People go on a diet to <u>lose</u> weight, but afterwards they often _____ the weight again.
2. If you <u>put on</u> a lot of weight, you may need to _____ it _____ again.
3. When I was a baby, I was <u>underweight</u>, so my parents were worried. They gave me so much to eat that I was soon _____ .

Speaking: talking about experience

You are going to find out about each other's experiences.
1. Work in pairs. Ask and answer these questions.

   - Have you ever tried a diet from the internet?
   - Have you heard of the cabbage soup diet?
   - Have you ever eaten snake?

2. What is the verb tense in the questions? How do we form it?
3. Write three similar types of questions.
4. Ask your questions to other students in the class. Find someone who says *yes* to your questions.
5. Tell the class what you found out.

> **Language tip**
> When we ask questions about experience, we often use the word *ever*.
>
> *Have you ever worried about your weight?*
>
> If the answer is positive, we can say: *Yes, I have.*
>
> If the answer is negative, we can use *never*: *No, and I've never been on a diet.*

deduce meaning of vocabulary; present perfect tense

How can we keep healthy?

Reading: what are they talking about?

1 Read what Lara and Alex say. What question do you think they were asked?

> Yes, I do worry about my weight. I don't want to be fat. I've been on a few diets but they don't really work. I lose some weight but then I put it back on after a few weeks. I try to eat healthy foods most of the time. I don't find this difficult because I love fruit and vegetables. My problem is that I also love chocolate! I've put on a few kilos recently. I think I might try a diet I saw on *YouTube* – lots of my friends are using it and say I should try it.

> No, I've never thought about my weight, or about what I eat. I eat anything and I've never been overweight. I think it's because I do so much exercise. I walk or run to school most days, I play football during breaks and at the weekend, and I play tennis and swim whenever I can. Oh yes, I go to the gym two or three times a week, too. This keeps me really fit and healthy. I don't eat sweets and cakes, either. They make you fat.

2 Read carefully what Lara says. Is what she says about diets clear?

3 Read carefully what Alex says. Is what he says about the food he eats clear?

> *Language tip*
> Sometimes when we speak, we are not sure what we want to say. We might say one thing, and then say something different, and this is OK. However, when we write, we should think more carefully and try to be clear. When we read, we should look out for when the writer is not clear.

Writing: how healthy are you?

1 Think about these questions.
- Do you try to eat healthy foods, like Lara?
- Do you love chocolate, like Lara?
- What's your favourite food?
- Do you eat lots of fruit and vegetables?
- Do you eat sweets and cakes?
- Do you do a lot of exercise, like Alex?
- Are you most like Lara or Alex in the way that you eat and exercise? How are you different?

2 Write an answer to the question: *Do you try to keep healthy?*
- Write about any healthy and unhealthy food that you eat.
- Write about any exercise that you do.

3 Work in pairs. Take turns to read out and discuss your answers to the question.

recognise inconsistencies in a text; write with moderate accuracy

Use of English: sentence adverbs

1 Look at these sentences that Alex uses. What are the missing words?
1. I go to the gym two or three times a week, _____
2. I don't eat sweets and cakes, _____

2 Choose the correct way to complete the sentences.
1. Sentence adverbs (like *too* and *either*) describe:
   - a the verb
   - b the first part of the sentence
   - c the whole sentence.
2. The sentence adverbs *too* and *either* go:
   - a at the beginning of the sentence
   - b in the middle of the sentence
   - c at the end of the sentence.
3. The word *too* means the same as *also*:
   - a in a positive sentence
   - b in a negative sentence.
4. The word *either* means the same as *also*:
   - a in a positive sentence
   - b in a negative sentence.

3 What is different about the sentence adverbs used in these sentences?

<u>Clearly</u>, Alex loves sports and exercise.

<u>Unfortunately</u>, we don't all have time to do so much exercise.

4 Work in pairs. Make sentences using the sentence adverbs in the box.

| also   certainly   clearly   either   too |

Reading: setting the scene

1 Discuss.
- What do you know about healthy eating?
- What should / shouldn't you eat and drink?
- What else do you need to do to keep healthy?

2 What would be your top five tips for healthy living?

Reading: understanding the main points

Read the text on page **126** and compare the tips with your own ones.

TOP TIPS ... for Healthy Living

Understanding all the information about health and healthy living isn't easy. Some people say we should eat this, others say don't eat that, some say we have to do one thing, others say we mustn't do another thing – it can be <u>confusing</u>.

So here are a few key points that everyone agrees on.

A key word is **balance**. The elephant and the mouse aren't happy because they're not balanced.

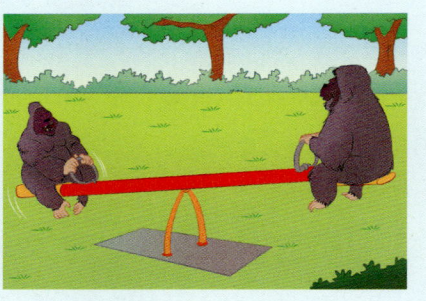

The gorilla and the orangutan are having fun because they are balanced.

- **Eat a balanced diet**. There are a lot of different types of food, and you should try to eat some of all types, but not too much of any one type. It's not wrong to eat a few sweets and chips, just try not to eat too many. Do eat plenty of fruit and vegetables – they're really good for you.

- **Eat when you're hungry and stop eating when you're not**. This tip is our favourite because it's so simple, but it's not easy to do. It means don't keep eating just because you enjoy something – balance what you enjoy with what your body needs.

- **Exercise for about 60 minutes a day**. You get energy from food, but you should balance this with the energy your body uses. If you take in more energy than you use, you'll put on weight. If you use more energy than you take in, you'll lose weight. (But don't make the mistake that you can eat what you want as long as you do a lot of exercise. You still need to eat a balanced diet.)

- **Get enough sleep**. This is very important for health and happiness. Children aged between 11 and 14 need around 9 to 9.5 hours of sleep a night.

- And finally, a surprising one! **Clean your teeth well** because problems in the mouth can cause serious illness. So, brush morning and night, and don't eat sugary food or drink before you go to bed.

Reading: thinking about the text

1. Read the tips. How good are you at following these tips? Give yourself a mark for each tip, from A to E (A is excellent, E is very bad).

2. Think of a question to ask about each tip, for example: *Do you have a balanced diet?*.

3. Work in pairs. Ask and answer your questions.

    Don't just answer *yes* or *no*. Explain your answers and give examples.

read for main points; deduce meaning from a text

Vocabulary: word building

Work in pairs. Discuss these questions.

1. When someone wants to help us, they can give us a *tip*. What's another word for a *tip*?
2. When people tell us one thing and then tell us something different, it can be *confusing*. What is the adjective to describe how we feel when something is confusing?
3. The word *balance* is a noun. How can we make it into an adjective?
4. Find a word in the third tip that means 'the power that your body needs to keep it working'.
5. What is an abstract noun? (See page 56 if you can't remember.) Find two abstract nouns in the fourth and fifth tips which end in *–ness*. What do these nouns mean?
6. The text says that the sixth tip is a *surprising* one. What is the adjective to describe how we feel when something is surprising?
7. The word *sugar* is a noun. How is it made into an adjective?

Use of English: using the *–ing* form

1 Look at first sentence of the text on page 126.
1. What is the main verb?
2. Is *understanding* used as a verb in this sentence?

2 Is *cycling* used as a verb or a noun in these sentences?
- *Cycling is good exercise.*
- *I enjoy cycling.*

3 Make sentences about what you like and don't like to do to keep healthy.
- *I enjoy swimming/playing tennis.*
- *I don't like eating cabbage soup.*

Writing: a lifestyle diary

1 Keep a diary for one day. Include all your food and drink, and all the exercise you do.

You can use Worksheet 11B.

2 Look again at *Top Tips … for Healthy Living* on page 126. Think about your own lifestyle. Write a few sentences about how healthy you think it is.

3 Now write few sentences about what you could do to have a lifestyle that is more healthy.

deduce meaning of vocabulary; gerunds as subjects and objects

Focus on Health Science

Nutrient food groups

A balanced diet contains different nutrients in the correct amounts to keep us healthy. There are five main nutrient groups found in food. We need all of them for a balanced diet.

Carbohydrates
give you energy

Proteins
help your body grow and repair itself

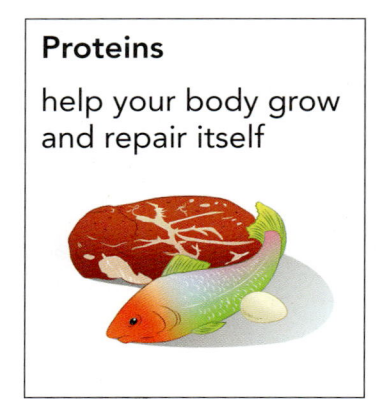

Fats
are needed to store energy

Vitamins
are needed in small quantities to keep the body working properly

Minerals
are needed in small quantities to keep the body working properly

To keep healthy, we also need **fibre** and **water**. Fibre keeps food moving through our bodies, and is found in fruit, vegetables and cereal. Water carries the nutrients around our bodies.

1 Copy and complete the table with information from the text.

Food group	What is it for?	Where is it found?
carbohydrates	1 _____	2 _____
3 _____	help the body to grow and repair itself	4 _____
5 _____	6 _____	oil, cheese, nuts
7 _____	keep the body working properly	8 _____
minerals	9 _____	10 _____
11 _____	keep food moving through the body	12 _____
13 _____	14 _____	fruit juice, tea, coffee

read for main points and specific information

2 Which way do you think shows the information more clearly, the cards and diagrams, or the table?

3 Match these words from the text with their meanings.

1 repair
2 store
3 properly
4 cereal

a a type of food (some people eat it for breakfast)
b in the correct way
c to fix something that is not working well
d to keep something to use later

Many foods <u>contain</u> more than one nutrient. For example, milk (and foods made from milk) contains protein, vitamins and minerals. Some foods contain a lot of one type of nutrient. For example, sweets are mostly sugar, which is a source of carbohydrate only.

The plate shows how to balance different types of foods, so that you can get all the nutrients you need.

4 Which are the two biggest sections on the plate?

5 Which is the smallest section? Why do you think we shouldn't eat too much of this type of food?

6 Work in pairs. Name as many of the foods on the plate as you can.

Which pair has the most words?

read for main points and specific information   129

Project: a healthy lifestyle questionnaire

In this project you are going to answer part of a lifestyle questionnaire and then develop one of your own.

1 Answer these questions.

a How much water should you drink each day?
  A 4–6 glasses
  B 6–8 glasses
  C 8–10 glasses

b What is the most important meal of the day?
  A breakfast
  B lunch
  C dinner

c How many teaspoons of sugar are there in a can of cola?
  A fewer than four
  B between five and eight
  C more than eight

2 Now check your answers. How well did you do?

3 Work in pairs. Write five more questions for the healthy lifestyle questionnaire.

- Think of questions about food, drink, exercise or anything else to do with a healthy lifestyle.
- Use information from this unit, or do some research to find out more.
- Write the questions on one piece of paper, and the answers on another piece of paper. Make sure you give an explanation for the answer.

4 Give your questions to another pair. Answer the questions they give you.

5 Tell each other the answers to your questions. Explain why each answer is correct.

6 Make a new healthy lifestyle questionnaire, with six questions to ask your friends and family. Choose from the questions you have asked and answered.

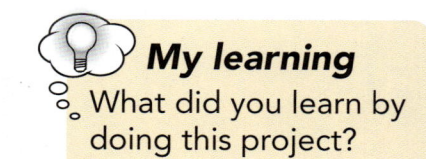

My learning
What did you learn by doing this project?

ANSWERS

a C It is important to drink plenty of water. If you do exercise or it is very hot, you should drink even more than this.

b A Breakfast gives you energy to start the day. If you don't eat a healthy breakfast you will get tired and hungry during the morning, and might then eat an unhealthy snack.

c C Try not to drink too many of these types of drinks as they contain a lot of sugar. It is much healthier to drink water.

interact with peers to negotiate a task

Game shows 12

Looking forward

This unit explores some game shows and will give you the chance to play some quiz games.

You will read
- about the world's most popular game show
- part of a story about a game show

You will listen
- to a game show, and then play the game
- to answer questions as part of some quiz games

You will speak
- to ask and answer questions as you play some quiz games

You will write
- a range of questions for quiz games

You will learn
- about adding meaning to sentences with phrases
- how to express wishes, using *I wish …* and *If only …*
- to use a wide range of questions

The world's favourite game show

Reading: setting the scene

Discuss.
- Which game shows do you know?
- Which is your favourite game show? What do you like about it?
- Can you answer this game show question?

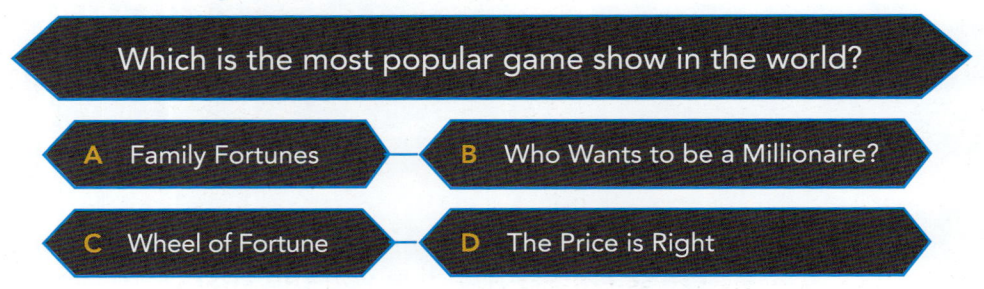

> Which is the most popular game show in the world?
>
> A Family Fortunes
> B Who Wants to be a Millionaire?
> C Wheel of Fortune
> D The Price is Right

Just type in a question and click Find Out!

| What is the most popular game show in the world? | **Find out!** |

Watched in more than a hundred countries, from Afghanistan to Vietnam, the world's favourite game show is *Who Wants to be a Millionaire?* It was first shown in 1998 and is still showing around the world.

In this show, there is just one player at a time. The player is asked a series of questions, which get more and more difficult. Each correct answer earns the player more and more money. All questions have four answers that the player can choose from. If the player can't answer a question, he or she can use a 'lifeline'. They have three different lifelines:

- 50 : 50 (the four answers are reduced to two)
- ask the audience (who use special machines to show their answers)
- phone a friend (to ask them for help).

When John Carpenter went on the game show in 1999, he reached the final question without using any lifelines. He then asked to telephone his father. However, he didn't need help but just wanted to tell his father that he was going to win the big prize! He answered the final question correctly and became the first million-dollar winner in the USA.

In 2001, a soldier in the British army, Major Ingram, won the million-pound prize. However, it was noticed by the makers of the show that someone in the audience coughed every time the correct answer was mentioned. The police were called, and Major Ingram, his wife and the friend in the audience were arrested. Major Ingram lost the prize money, and then lost his job because he was told to leave the army. He 'wanted to be a millionaire' a bit too much!

The game show has become so famous around the world that it was used for the plot of a book, *Q&A*. This book was then made into a very successful film called *Slumdog Millionaire*.

read for specific information

Reading: exploring the text

1 Look at the text. Where do you think it comes from?
   a the letter page of a newspaper
   b an advertisement
   c a question-and-answer website

2 Read the text. What is the answer to the last question in *Reading: setting the scene*?

Reading: understanding the text

Read the text again. Answer these questions.

1. How does a player win money in *Who Wants to Be a Millionaire*?
2. When does a player use a lifeline?
3. How do we know that John Carpenter was good at the game?
4. What was 'the big prize' that John Carpenter told his father about?
5. How did Major Ingram's friend help him to win the game?
6. What is a *millionaire*?

Vocabulary: words in context

Match these words from the text to the meanings below.

| series | audience | reached | soldier | army | noticed | coughed | successful |

1. a large group of people who are ready to fight wars on land
2. doing or getting what you want
3. found out about someone or something by seeing, hearing or feeling them
4. a group of the same things that come one after the other
5. got to a place or point
6. made a sudden noise by pushing air out of the mouth
7. someone who is in an army
8. the people who watch a play, show, film, TV programme, and so on.

features of a text; understand detail of an argument; deduce meaning

Use of English: adding meaning

1 **Look at these sentences from the text. Answer the questions.**

- It was first shown in 1998 and is still showing *around the world*.
- *In this show* there is just one player at a time.
- However, it was noticed *by the makers of the show* that someone in the audience coughed every time the correct answer was mentioned.

  1 Are the underlined words
     a adjectives   b prepositions   c conjunctions?
  2 The phrases in *italics* add meaning to the sentences. Do they add meaning in the same way as
     a verbs   b nouns   c adjectives and adverbs?
  3 Where do the phrases go in a sentence?
     a at the beginning   b in the middle   c at the end   d in any position
  4 Find one more example of these phrases in the sentences above.

2 **Make sentences using these phrases.**

> in the film   behind the door   at home   over the bridge

Language tip

You already know that using adjectives and adverbs in sentences helps to make your writing more interesting. They add meaning to nouns and verbs.

We can do the same thing by adding phrases of a few words or more.

Speaking: *wishes*

1 **Look at what Sara and Amy say. What are they talking about?**
  a what they plan to do
  b what they wish they could do

> I wish I could play *Who Wants to Be a Millionaire?* It would be fun.

> If only I could win a million dollars, I'd travel around the world.

2 **Imagine you have three wishes. What would they be?**

3 **Work in groups. Discuss your three wishes.**

> I wish I could …   I wish I was …   I wish I had a …   If only I could …

134   prepositional phrases; wish clauses

If this is the answer, what's the question?

Listening: can you guess?

You are going to listen to part of a quiz called, *If this is the answer, what's the question?*

1. 🔊 Listen to the first part to see how the quiz works.
2. What's the answer? What do you think the question is?
3. Listen to the second part. What help does the woman give? Now what do you think the question is?
4. Listen to the final part. What was the question?

Vocabulary: words in context

Read these sentences from the quiz show. Match the words and phrases in bold to the meanings below.

1 Now you're being **silly**.
2 It **has nothing to do with** weight.
3 It's a question about **speed**.
4 Joan wins the **point**.

a   a number you use to count the score in a game or sport
b   how fast something moves or travels
c   is about something different from
d   not serious, clever or intelligent

Use of English: questions

1 🔊 Listen again to the quiz show. Copy and complete these questions.
   1 Did _____ 75?
   2 _____ guess?
   3 _____ hours of sleep do we need each week?
   4 _____ will I weigh if I eat only burgers?
   5 _____ a question about speed?

listen for specific information; question forms

2 **Look at the five questions you have written in activity 1 above. Answer these questions.**
   1. Which questions can we answer *yes* or *no*?
   2. Which question is about the past? Which word tells us?
   3. Which question is asking about ability? Which word tells us?
   4. Which questions include question words?
   5. Which other question words do you know?

3 **Follow the instructions and answer the questions.**
   1. Change these sentences into questions.
      a It is about a plane.　　b You can help.

      What did you do to make questions?
   2. Change these sentences into questions with *yes* or *no* answers.
      a He weighs a lot.　　b She said 75.

      What did you do to make questions?
   3. Look at these answers. What are the questions?
      a It's six o'clock.　　b I'm 13.　　c He went to see the nurse.

      What did you do to make questions?

4 **Work in a group. Play *If this is the answer, what is the question?***
   Think of a question. Take turns to say your answer and to guess the questions.

Blockbusters

Listening: play a game

Play *Blockbusters* in teams. Your teacher will ask the questions.

Writing: questions

Work in pairs. You are going to prepare to play a game called *Blockbusters*.

- Copy the *Blockbusters* grid below. (Put a sheet of paper over it and draw the lines you see.)

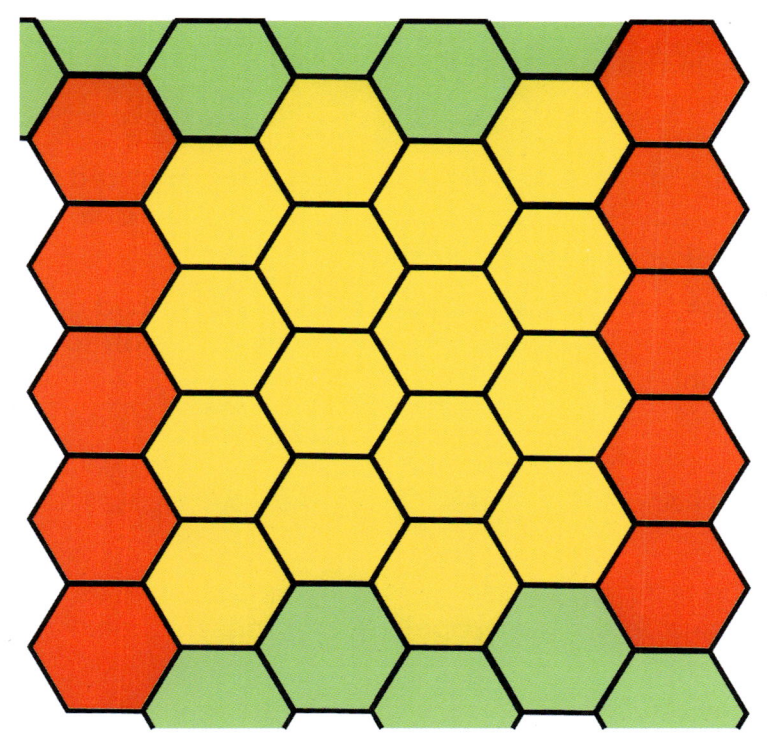

- Write a letter in each space. Use the most common letters. Don't use X.
- Think of a question for each letter. Write down the questions and the answers on a piece of paper. The answers to your questions must start with the letters in the blocks.
- Check that you have written your questions correctly.

Speaking: play *Blockbusters*

Work in groups of four. Follow these instructions to play the game.

- The first pair reads out their clues. The second pair plays against each other using the grid.
- Change roles.

listen for specific information; writing and asking questions

Focus on Literature

Q&A

You are going to read part of a book called *Q&A* by the Indian writer Vikas Swarup. *Q&A* means *questions and answers*. This story is about a man called Ram Mohammed Thomas who won a television quiz show.

1 Look at this picture. What is happening?

2 Find these items in the picture.

a handcuffs   b a jeep   c a flashing red light

3 Read the first part of the story. Why has Ram been arrested?

> I have been arrested. For winning a quiz show.
>
> They came for me late last night, when even the stray dogs had gone off to sleep. They broke open my door, handcuffed me and marched me off to the waiting jeep with a flashing red light.

Study tip

Many stories are told using the third person, for example: *He was arrested. They came for him late at night.*

This one is told in the first person, using *I, me, my*, and so on. This helps the writer tell the character's thoughts, feelings and opinions as things happen.

4 Read the next part quickly (don't try to understand every word). Does Ram think he has been arrested because he is

a a waiter   b a restaurant owner   c poor   d rich?

> There are those who will say that I brought this upon myself. By dabbling in that quiz show. They will wag a finger at me and remind me of what the elders in Dharavi say about never crossing the dividing line that separates the rich from the poor. After all, what business did a penniless waiter have to be participating in a brain quiz? The brain is not an organ we are authorised to use. We are supposed to use only our hands and legs.
>
> If only they could see me answer those questions. After my performance they would have looked upon me with new respect. It's a pity the show has yet to be telecast. But word seeped out that I had won something. Like a lottery. When the other waiters heard the news they decided to have a big party for me in the restaurant. We sang and danced and drank late into the night. For the first time we did not eat Ramzi's stale food for dinner. We ordered chicken biryani and seekh kebabs from the five-star hotel in Marine Drive.

read a fiction text

5 Read again the text in **4** above. Choose the sentences that describe what Ram is thinking. Use the *Word help* section to understand any difficult words.

1. a Some people think he shouldn't have taken part in a television quiz show.
   b Some people think he is very clever to take part in a television quiz show.
2. a The poor are stupid.
   b The rich want the poor to be stupid.
3. a People would think he was clever if they saw him answer the questions in the quiz.
   b People would think he was stupid if they saw him answer the questions in the quiz.
4. a The other waiters were angry he had won the big prize.
   b The other waiters were happy he had won the big prize.

Word help

I brought this upon myself – I made it happen
dabbling – playing around with something for a short time
wag a finger at me – get angry with me
remind me of what the elders in Dharavi say – make me remember what the old people in our area say
penniless – having no money
participating in a brain quiz – doing a quiz that needs thinking about
organ – part of the body that does a job (for example, the heart or the brain)
authorised – allowed, have permission
looked upon me with new respect – see me as someone clever or important
telecast – shown on television
seeped out – came out
stale – old and dry

6 A lawyer tries to help Ram. She asks him how he won the big prize. Read the conversation to find out.

'I got lucky on the show.'

'You mean you just guessed the answers and by pure luck got 12 out of 12 correct?'

'No. I didn't guess those answers. I knew them.'

'You *knew* the answers?'

'Yes. To all the questions.'

'Then where does luck come into the picture?'

'Well, wasn't I lucky that they only asked those questions to which I knew the answers?'

In the rest of the book, Ram tells the lawyer about his life. He has had a difficult life and had many adventures, but in each one he learned something new. The questions asked in the quiz were all about those things he learned. So he did know all the answers, but he was lucky that they asked the right questions.

7 This is one of the questions that Ram knew the answer to. Do you know the answer?

> What is the capital of Papua New Guinea?

8 Work in pairs. Discuss how you think Ram had learned the answer to the question. Did he travel there? Did he meet someone from there? What happened?

9 Work in groups. Tell one another your ideas about Ram's adventure.

read for main points; specific information; deduce meaning; recognise attitude

Project: Who Wants to Be a Millionaire?

In this project you are going to prepare and play a game of *Who Wants to Be a Millionaire?*

1 Work in groups. Write questions and answers for the game. Follow these instructions.

- Use 12 separate sheets of paper.
- On each sheet of paper, write a question, with one correct answer and three incorrect answers.
- Write a list of all the correct answers on a different sheet of paper.
- When the group has 12 questions, decide on the order of difficulty.
  - You need some easy questions (like Question 1 below) for the first questions.
  - You need some medium questions (like Question 2 below) for the questions in the middle.
  - You need some difficult questions (like Question 3 below) for the last questions.

1 A dragon fish is a type of _____.
   a bird   b insect
   c fish   d dragon

2 The ingredients in food that keep people healthy are _____.
   a nations   b nutrients
   c nuts   d neighbours

3 Nouns that are ideas, feelings or thoughts are called _____.
   a abstract   b unclear
   c general   d unusual

50:50	
12	$1 MILLION
11	$500.000
10	$250.000
9	$150.000
8	$75.000
7	$50.000
6	$20.000
5	$10.000
4	$5.000
3	$2.000
2	$1.000
1	$500

2 Play the game in two teams. Follow these instructions.

- Team A plays first. Players take turns to answer each of the questions.
- Players in Team B take turns to ask the questions.
- If a player can't answer, they can use a lifeline. Each lifeline can only be used once. There are two lifelines:
  - 50:50 (The team asking the questions must say two of the answers that are incorrect – leaving one incorrect and one correct answer.)
  - Ask the team (The player can ask his / her team to help.)
- Other players in the teams must stay quiet while questions are asked and answered (except during the *Ask the team* lifeline).
- If any player gives an incorrect answer, his / her team is out.

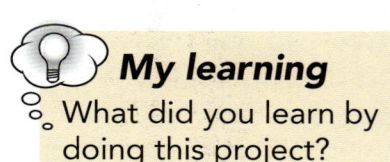

My learning
What did you learn by doing this project?

Review 5

> **Study tip**
> It's review time again!

Speaking: looking back

Look back through Units 11 and 12.

1. Which activity did you enjoy the most? Say why you liked it and what you learned from doing it.
2. Find one photo you like. Say why you like it.

Reading: asking questions

Look back through Units 11 and 12. If these are the answers, what are the questions?

1. About 95%.   *How many people put on weight after a diet?*
2. Something in food that keeps people healthy.
3. I need about nine hours a night.
4. carbohydrates
5. breakfast
6. for winning a quiz show

Listening: what's missing?

1. **This is part of the talk about diets which you listened to in Unit 11. Think about questions and phrases that can fill the gaps 1–6.**

   Let me start with a question. ¹_____ You know what I mean, a special diet in which you eat some foods and don't eat others, with the aim of losing weight quickly. ²_____

   Well, before you guess and then want me to give the correct answer, let me tell you that ³_____ There's one health website that lists more than 150, but people keep coming up with new ones. ⁴_____ Well, to use most of them, you need to buy a book, video or the special foods for the diet. So the people behind the diets can make ⁵_____ In fact, the diet business around the world is worth around ⁶_____ – that's more money than all but the 40 richest countries make in a year.

2. 🔊 **Now listen, and write down the missing questions and phrases.**

Vocabulary: *Countdown*

A popular quiz show is *Countdown*. In this show, people are given some letters and they try to make the longest word possible with those letters.
What's the longest word you can make from these letters?

COUNTDOWN

SYFELTILE

Use of English: talking about experiences

1. Think about some of the great things that have happened in your life. They may be things you have done or seen, places you have been to, or people you have met.
2. Have you ever done something that wasn't good, or that you didn't like?
3. Work in a group. Tell one another about your experiences.

> The best thing I've done in my life is …

> I've seen …

> I've been to …

> The worst thing I've ever done is …

Use of English: a game

You are going to work in teams to play a game called *Blankety Blank*. Your teacher will read out sentences that contain the word BLANK to show a missing word. Write down what you think is the best word to complete the sentence.

Have you ever BLANK a snake?   The word could be **seen**, **eaten** or even **met**.

Speaking: a conversation

1. Look at the picture. What do you think the people are talking about?
2. Work in pairs. Write some questions you think they might be asking.
3. Then work in a group. Ask and answer one another's questions.

Writing: a conversation

Write a conversation using the questions and answers you discussed in 3 above.

Writing: three wishes

1. Work in pairs. If you had three wishes, what would they be? Discuss.

> I wish I could …

> If only I could …

> I'd like to …

> I'd love to …

2. Write sentences about your wishes.

   For each wish, explain why it is important to you.
   I wish I could fly so that I could go wherever I want and see the world below me.

Rivers and bridges 13

Looking forward

This unit explores some famous bridges and some of the great rivers of the world.

You will read
- a travel blog about a river journey
- about ancient Egypt

You will listen
- to descriptions of three bridges and identify them in photos

You will speak
- about a traveller's plans for a journey down the River Nile
- about plans to make your own river journey as part of a project

You will write
- a blog post about a journey
- a plan of a river journey, as part of a project

You will learn
- about the past continuous tense and when to use it
- about the past perfect tense and when to use it

Favourite bridges

Listening: setting the scene

Discuss.

- Is there a big or famous bridge in your area? Where is it? What does it go over?
- Do you have a favourite bridge? Where is it? Why do you like it?
- Look at the photos of bridges on pages 143 and 144. Which do you like the most? Why?

Listening: for detail

🔊 14 Listen to three people answering the question, *Do you have a favourite bridge?* Which bridge (A–D) are they talking about?

A

B

C

D

144   *listen for detail*

Vocabulary: words in context

Look at these words from the listening passage and answer the questions.

1 … *they didn't use any nails.* Which one is a nail?

   a   b   c

2 … *the old bridge was <u>destroyed</u> in a war …* What does *destroyed* mean?
   a   broken by someone or something so that it cannot be used again
   b   broken because of age and use

3 *It's … not very long because it crosses a narrow river …* What is *narrow* the opposite of?
   a   long   b   deep   c   wide

Use of English: past continuous tense

1 Look at these sentences from the listening passage. What is the name of the verb tense?

> I was visiting.   I was walking.   They were jumping.

2 Read the *Language tip* box. Look at the sentences in the box above and write a description of the past continuous tense.

3 How do we make these sentences negative?

4 How do we change these sentences into questions?

5 Read and then play the game, *What were you doing at 7 o'clock last night?*

> *Language tip*
> The present continuous tense:
>
> is used to talk about actions that are continuing in the present
>
> is made with *am / is / are* + *–ing* form of the verb.
>
> *I am reading.*
> *The teacher is talking.*
> *We are working.*

> At 7 o'clock last night I was watching TV. What were you doing, Sara?

> While Anna was watching TV, I was talking to my father. What were you doing, Kate?

> While Anna was watching TV and Sara was talking to her father, I was reading a magazine. What were you doing, Paula?

past continuous tense

The River Nile

Speaking: making plans

Anton is planning a journey. Read what he says and look at his map.

> I've always dreamed of travelling along the Nile, from the beginning to the end. Now I'm planning the trip of a lifetime with my best friend, Carl.

Discuss.
1 Where is he going?
2 Where is he going to start and end his journey?
3 How do you think he will travel?
4 Which countries will he pass through?
5 What do you think he will see?
6 What do you think he will enjoy the most?
7 What might he find hard?
8 Would you like to go on this journey? Why / Why not?

interact to negotiate a task

Reading: exploring the text

1. Look at the text below. Where would you find this kind of text? What is it called?
2. Where were the three texts written? Find these places on the map.
3. When were they written? How long did the whole journey take?

Reading tip

Sometimes we have an opinion about something, but then something happens and we change our opinion. It's useful to look out for when a writer changes their opinion in a text.

Can you find in the blog where Anton changes his opinion about something?

Lake Victoria 25 January

This amazing journey to follow the Nile from beginning to end has started. We spent the first week walking, which was tiring, but we arrived at the boat last night. We had been to see where the Nile starts in the mountains of Burundi. We then followed it down to Lake Victoria. I'm now on a ferry crossing the lake, so I have time to relax and write.

The next part of the journey will take us through part of Uganda and into South Sudan. I'm looking forward to sitting in the boat and watching the world go by.

Khartoum 18 February

I'm really happy to arrive in a city and get off the boat. The last few weeks have been very difficult. In South Sudan the river flows slowly through a very flat area. It was extremely hot, with many flies and mosquitoes. But now we can walk the streets and go inside restaurants to get cool.

However, I shouldn't complain because most of the journey has been really good. In Uganda we saw hippos and huge Nile crocodiles, and many large birds I can't name.

Alexandria 18 March

We reached the Mediterranean yesterday, so the journey is over! Last week we were in Cairo, which was a great experience. It's an incredible mix of old and new. The modern city is full of international banks, offices and shops, but just behind them are the narrow streets of the market, which hasn't changed in 600 years. It was very crowded and noisy, so I missed the peace and quiet we had enjoyed on the boat.

Of course, before we got to Cairo we had also visited the famous pyramids. They were fantastic but there were too many tourists!

---

typical features of a text; recognise opinion and inconsistency

Reading: understanding the text

Read the blog posts and answer the questions.
1. On which date did Anton and Carl arrive at the boat?
2. What did they do before they arrived at the boat?
3. On 25 January, what does Anton think about the boat journey through Uganda and South Sudan that he is about to start?
4. On 18 February, what does he think now about the boat journey through South Sudan?
5. On 8 March, he says visiting Cairo was 'a great experience'. Was there anything he didn't like?
6. Does Anton prefer looking quietly at wildlife or visiting busy places? How do you know?

Vocabulary: words in context

1 Find these words in the text and match them to their meaning.

1. relax
2. flow
3. extremely
4. complain
5. mix

a. something made by putting two or more things together
b. to move at all times
c. to rest quietly
d. to talk about something that you are not happy with
e. very

2 Find the following phrases in the text and choose the correct meaning.

1. *looking forward to* means:
   a. feeling happy and excited about something that is going to happen
   b. looking at what is happening in front of you
2. *watching the world go by* means:
   a. travelling to look at interesting places
   b. sitting quietly and looking at what is passing by
3. *peace and quiet* means:
   a. a boring situation, with is nothing to do
   b. a quiet situation, with is no noise from other people

3 Look in the blog posts to find the names of two insects. Match the names to these pictures.

A   B

Use of English: past perfect tense

1 Look at the blog posts and the map. Put these six events in the correct order.
   a arrived in Alexandria
   b arrived in Cairo
   c arrived in Khartoum
   d got on a ferry at Lake Victoria
   e visited the pyramids
   f visited the source of the Nile

2 Look at these sentences from the blog posts and answer the questions.
   1 On 25 January, Anton wrote, *we had been to see where the Nile starts*.
      Did he see where the Nile starts before or after he got on the ferry?
   2 On 18 March, he wrote about Cairo and said, *I missed the peace and quiet we had enjoyed on the boat*.
      Did he enjoy the peace and quiet on the boat before or after he visited Cairo?
   3 On 18 March, he wrote about Cairo and said, *we had also visited the famous pyramids*.
      Did he visit the pyramids before or after he went to Cairo?

3 Look at the underlined verbs in activity 2 above. They are in the past perfect tense.
   1 Is this the same as the past simple tense (for example, *went, enjoyed, visited*)?
   2 How is this tense formed?
   3 Is it used to talk about a time before the past or about a time before the future?

4 Talk about things you *had done*.

> What had you done before you arrived at school today?

> I had eaten breakfast.

> I had finished my homework.

Writing: a blog post

Write a blog post about a journey you made, or about one you wish you had made.
The journey is now finished. Think about:
- some of the places you went to
- what you saw there
- what you enjoyed
- what you didn't enjoy.

Use Anton's blog posts as a model. Begin like this:

PLACE   DATE

The journey is over …

past perfect tense; plan, draft and develop a blog post

Focus on History

Ancient Egypt

1 Work in groups. Discuss what you know about ancient Egypt.

A

B

The Great Sphinx and pyramids at Giza

Hieroglyphics - early writing

C

Part of a wall painting, about 3200 years old

2 Look at photo C of the wall painting to learn about life in Ancient Egypt. What does it tell us about

- clothing
- work
- food
- agriculture?

3 Look at the information below. What does it show?

Timeline of ancient Egyptian civilisation

pre-Kingdom 5500–3100BCE	Early Egypt 3100–2600BCE	Old Kingdom 2600–2100BCE	Middle Kingdom 2100–1650BCE	New Kingdom 1650–1075BCE	Late Period 1075–30BCE
Upper and Lower Egypt were two nations.	Upper and Lower Egypt unite. Begin to use hieroglyphics.	Begin to build pyramids. Great Pyramid and Sphinx built.	Pyramid building stops. Osiris the most important god.	Kings buried in tombs.	The Romans take over Egypt (30BCE).

read for main points

4 Match the words from the timeline above with their meanings.

1 join together
2 countries
3 a society that has its own culture and way of life
4 a country ruled by a king or queen
5 a large place where a body is buried
6 a male spirit that people pray to and that has control over parts of the world or nature

a civilisation
b kingdom
c nations
d unite
e god
f tomb

5 Read this text. Make notes about all the ways in which the River Nile was important during ancient Egyptian civilisation.

Ancient Egypt and the River Nile

For the ancient Egyptians, the Nile was 'the father of life' and 'the mother of all men'. One of their favourite gods was Hapi, the god of the Nile. Every year they gave thanks to Hapi when the river flooded. Usually we would think of a flood as a bad thing, but for the ancient Egyptians it was extremely important. The floods brought water to the land and left behind thick, black mud that made the soil rich and good for growing crops. They called this mud the 'gift of the Nile'. Even today, nearly all of the population of Egypt lives close to the river, as most of the country is desert and there is very little rain. However, near the river there is water and the soil is fertile.

Did you know …?
The ancient Egyptians thought that the Nile floods were caused by the goddess Isis crying for her dead husband Osiris.

The floods were really caused by heavy rain and snow in the mountains of Ethiopia.

Today the Aswan dam stops the River Nile from flooding.

The ancient Egyptians farmed the land close to the river and caught fish in its waters. The mud from the floods was used for making buildings. Reeds, a kind of tall grass that grew in the river, were used for making baskets, sandals and even paper to write on.

The river was also used for transport, communication and trade between the different parts of the ancient Egyptian kingdom. The river was always busy. Boats sailed between the north and the south of the kingdom, carrying people and products to buy and sell.

6 Find words in the text that mean the following. The first letter is given to help you.

1 a large amount of water covering an area that is usually dry   f___
2 very soft wet earth   m___
3 the top of the ground, where plants grow   s___
4 when soil is able to produce good crops and plants   f___
5 light shoes that are partly open at the top   s___
6 the buying and selling of products   t___
7 moving over the water, using the wind   s___
8 a female god   g___
9 a large wall built across a river   d___

read extended non-fiction

Project: a river adventure

In this project you are going to work in groups to plan a river journey.

1. The diagram shows ten great rivers of the world. Find out where they are on a map. Choose which river you would like to visit.

Euphrates, Mekong, Yangtze, Zambezi, Amazon, Mississippi, Ganges, Danube, Volga, Congo

2. Do some research. Look at maps, websites and reference books to find out information you will need to know before you go on your river journey.

3. Discuss and decide about your group's answers to these questions.

   - Where will you start the journey?
   - How will you get to the starting point?
   - How will you travel along the river?
   - What will you take with you?
   - What will you see along the river?
   - What will you stop to visit?
   - How long will the journey take?
   - Where will the journey end?

4. Make a poster to show the plan of your river journey. You can add a map and some photos.

5. Prepare and give a talk about your river journey.

6. Look at other groups' posters, listen to the talks and ask questions. Who has planned the most exciting journey?

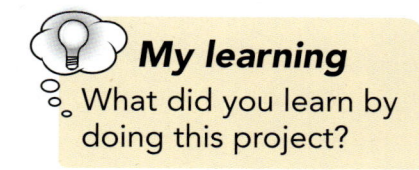

My learning
What did you learn by doing this project?

Hobbies 14

Looking forward

This unit explores some strange and new hobbies.

You will read
- about some very strange hobbies
- about four hobbies from different parts of the world

You will listen
- to instructions about how to create a soap carving

You will speak
- about different hobbies and activities
- about a favourite hobby and encourage others to do it
- with a group to research and give a talk about a new school club

You will write
- an introduction for a website about a favourite hobby
- instructions to do something

You will learn
- about using relative clauses to add information to sentences
- about when to use the *–ing* form and *to* + infinitive in sentences

Strange hobbies

Speaking: what's your hobby?

Discuss.
- What's your favourite hobby?
- How often do you spend time on your hobby?
- Would you like to spend time on your hobby every day? Why / Why not?
- Put these hobbies in order from most interesting (1) to least interesting (5).

    skydiving   stamp collecting   yoga   sewing   playing squash

- Which other hobbies would you like to try? Why?
- Which hobbies would you never want to do? Why?
- Can you think of any strange hobbies?

Reading: exploring the text

1 Work in pairs. Look at the headings and the photos in the text. Discuss answers to these questions.
- What do the words *ironing* and *grooming* mean?
- What is *extreme ironing*?
- What happens at *dog grooming competitions*?
- What is *dirty car art*?

2 Now read the text to check your answers.

Reading: understanding the writer's attitude

1 **Extreme ironing**

Read the first paragraph. Is it meant to be funny or serious?

2 **Dog grooming competitions**
1. Does the writer think that dog grooming is strange?
2. Does the writer think that dog grooming competitions are strange?
3. What in the text tells you the answers to questions 1 and 2?

read for implied meaning and attitude

3 Dirty car art
1. Does the writer think that making art out of dirty car windows is a good idea?
2. Which words tell you this?

4 What is the writer trying to do in this text?
a to make you want to try the hobbies
b to interest and amuse you
c to teach you about some important hobbies

The strangest hobbies

Do you have a hobby? Well, we're sure it's not as strange as these three!

Extreme ironing

Do you enjoy extreme sports? Do you like smart, well-ironed clothes? If yes, then extreme ironing could be for you!

The hobby, which began in the UK in 1997, became so popular that in 2002 it had its own World Championships in Germany. Extreme ironists (this is what they call themselves) have ironed their shirts in canoes, on mountain tops, on skis and even during a skydive. In 2011 a group of 173 divers won the record for the largest group of people ironing underwater. More recently, the man who invented the hobby ran a 21-kilometre race while carrying his ironing board and ironing all the way!

Dog grooming competitions

We all need a haircut from time to time. It's the same with long-haired dogs. This is where dog groomers come in – but quite why dog grooming *competitions* began, I'm not sure. At these competitions, the groomers change their dogs into extraordinary creatures. It takes quite some time to do, but the results can be surprising!

Dirty car art

American artist Scott Wade has certainly found himself a special hobby – and a very creative one! Have you ever seen a really dirty car and written a message in the dust? Well, Scott has turned this same idea into art. After many years of practise, he has found ways to change dirty cars into mobile art galleries!

read for implied meaning and attitude

Vocabulary: words in context

1 On page **64** we looked at compound words such as *skydiving*. There are a few compound words in this text.

1 Find a compound adverb that describes where people have ironed.
2 Find a compound noun that is the name of something people iron on.
3 Find a compound adjective that describes some kinds of dogs.

2 Find the word *smart* at the beginning of the text about extreme ironing. It is a word with more than one meaning. Which meaning is used in the text?

a clean and tidy, with nice clothes
b clever; intelligent
c using computer technology (for example, *a smartphone*)

3 Find words in the texts that mean the following:

Extreme ironing

1 a competition to find the best player or team
2 created or thought of something new

Dog grooming competitions

3 very special or strange

Dirty car art

4 using a lot of imagination and new ideas
5 very small pieces of dirt in the air and on top of furniture.
6 easy to move and use in different places

Use of English: relative clauses

1 The underlined part of this sentence is a type of relative clause you studied on pages **54** and **55**.

The hobby, which began in the UK in 1997, became so popular that in 2002 it had its own World Championships in Germany.

1 If we take out the underlined clause, is this still a correct sentence?
2 What punctuation goes before the clause and after the clause?

2 These sentences about the text use a different type of relative clause.

*The man **who** invented this form of painting found a way to create a mobile art gallery.*

*A mobile art gallery is one **which** moves around.*

*A dog groomer is someone **that** cuts a dog's hair.*

*Paintings **that** are done on dusty car windows are called dirty car art.*

compound nouns; refining relative clauses

1 If we take out the underlined clauses, are they all good sentences?
2 Do we use commas in these kinds of relative clauses?

3 Look at the first words (called relative pronouns) of the relative clauses in the sentences in activity 2 above.

1 Do we use *who* to refer to people or things?
2 Do we use *which* to refer to people or things?
3 Do we use *that* to refer to people or things, or both?

Language tip
This kind of relative clause tells us important information about a noun. It is a key part of the sentence.

4 Think of ways to complete these sentences. Then work in pairs and compare.

I like people who …

I dislike people that …

I hate films that …

I like TV programmes which …

Soap carving

Listening: setting the scene

1 Look at the big photo on the first page of this unit.

1 What are the flowers made of?
2 Have you ever heard of *soap carving*? What do you know about it?

2 Imagine that you are making a fish by carving a piece of soap. Put these pictures in the correct order.

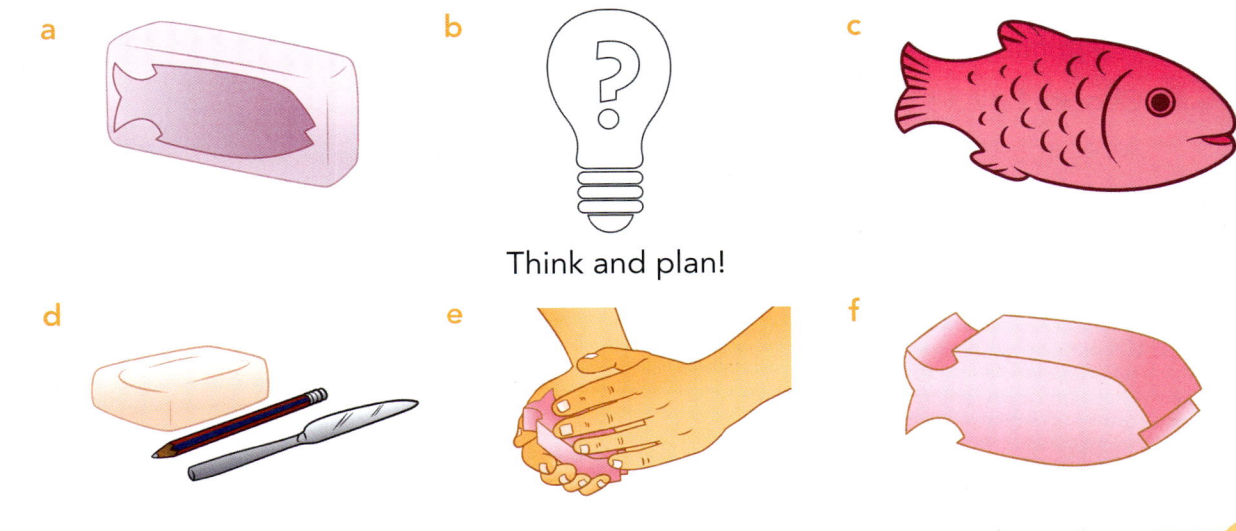

a

b
Think and plan!

c

d

e

f

defining relative clauses 157

Listening: instructions

1 🔊 **Listen to the whole talk. Answer these questions.**
  1 How many objects are required to make a soap carving?
  2 How many steps are involved in making a soap carving?

2 **Find the meaning of the words in the box. Make sentences about soap carving, using these words.**

> design   outline   shape   rough   smooth   rub   details

3 **Read and copy this instruction sheet for soap carving. Can you complete the missing parts?**

4 **Listen to the talk again. Complete the instructions.**

5 **Listen once more. Check that you completed the instructions correctly.**

> Soap carving: instructions
> What you need: soap   ª ____ knife (or spoon)
> What you do: 1 ᵇ ____ your carving.
>   2 ᶜ ____ of your design on the soap.
>   3 ᵈ ____ Do it carefully!
>   4 ᵉ ____ to make it smooth.
>   5 Wet the soap and ᶠ ____ .

Use of English: –ing form and to + verb

> **Language tip**
> Sometimes we have to choose between using the –ing form and to + verb (for example, *carving* or *to carve*).

1 **Read the Language tip box. Then answer these questions about adjectives followed by verbs.**
  1 Which is the correct example from the talk you listened to?
     a Soap carving is not <u>difficult doing</u>.
     b Soap carving is not <u>difficult to do</u>.
  2 Which are the correct sentences?
     a It's <u>dangerous driving</u> fast.
     b It's <u>dangerous to drive</u> fast.
     c I'm <u>happy hearing</u> you're better now.
     d I'm <u>happy to hear</u> you're better now.
  3 Choose how to complete this rule:
     After adjectives, we use [the –ing form / to + verb].

2 **Answer these questions about verbs followed by other verbs.**
  1 One instruction from the talk was, 'Start cutting the soap.' Can we also say, 'Start to cut the soap'?
  2 Which of these examples are correct?
     a I enjoy learning new hobbies.
     b I enjoy to learn new hobbies.
     c We're waiting buying some soap.
     d We're waiting to buy some soap.

listen for typical features, specific information and main points

3 Work in pairs. Copy and complete this table, using the verbs in the box. Make example sentences to help you.

begin finish imagine learn like plan prefer suggest want

verbs followed by –ing form	verbs followed by to + verb	verbs followed by either
		began

I began painting. I began to paint. They're both correct, so *began* can be followed by either.

My hobbies

Speaking: encouraging

1 Prepare to talk about one of your hobbies. Make notes about:
- what the hobby is
- what you need for the hobby, and how you do it
- why you think it is a good hobby.

2 Work in groups. Take turns to talk about your hobby and to encourage others to do it.

> *Encouraging people to do something*
>
> It's an excellent way to spend your time because …   I'd encourage you to try …
>
> You should try it!   Why don't you give it a try?   I think it's great!

Writing: introducing a hobby

1 Write about your hobby for a website about favourite hobbies. Make your text interesting and encourage readers to try the hobby.
- Introduce the hobby – what it is, how easy or difficult it is, and so on.
- Explain what is needed for the hobby, and a bit about how you do it.
- Explain what skills you need to do the hobby.
- Explain why people enjoy the hobby and why the reader should try it.

2 Work in groups. Read one another's texts. Then discuss these questions.
- Would you like to try any of the hobbies? Why / Why not?
- Who wrote the best description? How did he / she encourage you to try the hobby?

My learning

Think about the text you wrote and what your group said when they read it.

How could you make your text better?

compose, edit and proofread a text with coherent arguments

Focus on the World

1 Before you read, look at the pictures and the headings. What do you know about these types of hobbies?

Hobbies around the world

Kite flying

Kites are an invention of the Chinese, who first flew them more than 2000 years ago. The idea of kites travelled from China to Korea, and then across Asia to India. Each culture developed its own type and design of kite. These days, there are kite festivals in India, Japan and other parts of Asia and North America.

Anyone can fly a kite – here are a few tips:

- Find a big open space for flying. You don't want to be near buildings or trees, or too many people.
- You need wind, so a quiet day is not good, but neither is a very windy day because you will find it difficult to control your kite.
- Before you fly your kite, check it carefully. Make sure nothing is broken.
- Ask a friend to help you get the kite into the air.

Happy flying!

Calligraphy

Calligraphy means 'beautiful writing' and is the art of forming beautiful shapes on paper. It has been described as the closest you can get to hearing music with your eyes.

It developed from more than one culture. Early examples have been found in China, from more than 4000 years ago. Egyptian hieroglyphics are another early example of calligraphy. Later, it developed as an important part of Arabic, Japanese and some European civilisations.

Calligraphy was, and still is, an art form. It's a way to communicate through words, shape and design, all at the same time. Many people still do it – all it needs are some pens or brushes, paper, and the time to learn and practise.

160 read extended non-fiction

Metal toy art

This hobby is quite new, but comes from a long history of children making their own toys out of whatever they could find. Children who didn't have expensive toys would make things to play with out of sticks, stones and leaves and, more recently, they started to recycle rubbish from the modern world. An empty tin can become a bus or a lorry. A bottle top can make a steering wheel for a car. Some old wire can become a bike wheel.

At first, kids in South Africa made these toys for fun, but they have now become something more.

Tourists saw the toys and wanted to take them home for their own children to play with. So, when these South African children grew up, they continued with their hobby and turned it into a business. Nowadays these toys made out of recycled rubbish that can be bought around the world and seen in art galleries.

Word help

metal – a hard shiny substance that is used to make things (for example, spoons, cars, planes)

wire – a long thin piece of metal (electricity can pass through it)

Ice skating

It is thought that the very first ice skates were used around 5000 years ago in Finland and were made of animal bones.

Ice skating is still very popular in the northern countries of the world. Special places for skating, called ice rinks, open in winter, but some people love to skate outside on rivers and lakes.

It takes a bit of time to learn to balance on your skates, but once you can, it can be great fun. Why not give it a go if you get the chance?

Word help

bone – one of the hard parts inside a body

2 Read the text. Then copy and complete this table.

	Kite flying	Calligraphy	Metal toy art	Ice skating
Where it first started				
When it first started				
What is needed or used				

3 Match these words and phrases from the text with their meanings.

1. develop
2. control
3. recycle
4. become something more
5. give it a go if you get the chance

a. to change or grow
b. to get more important
c. to make something work in the way you want
d. to try [something] if you can
e. to use again (often in a different way)

4 If you could do one of these four hobbies, which one would you choose? Why?

read extended non-fiction

Project: a new hobby

Your school has the money to start one new club. In groups, you are going to decide about a new hobby or sports activity for this club, and then persuade other students to support your idea.

1 In your group, choose a suitable hobby or sports activity. Look at the diagram for ideas and also think of your own ideas. Do *not* choose a hobby or sports activity that is already done in your school – it must be NEW!

pottery, birdwatching, sewing, rock climbing, blogging, gardening, fishing, cooking, painting, yoga, candle making, drama, jewellery making, woodworking, collecting coins

2 Research your hobby / activity. You will need to find out:
- what is needed to do it
- how you do it, how difficult it is, and so on.
- what is enjoyable about it, what you can learn from doing it, and so on.
- any other reasons you think will help persuade others to support your idea.

3 Prepare a presentation about your hobby / activity. Apart from describing it, you could also:
- show how it is done
- show photos of people doing it
- show a real object or a photo of something that was made or done as a result of the hobby / activity.

4 Listen to the group talks. Ask questions to find out more about each hobby / activity.

My learning
What did you learn by doing this project?

5 Decide which hobby / activity is the best choice for your school's new club.

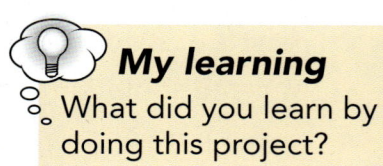

use reference resources; interact to negotiate a task

Review 6

> *Study tip*
> It's review time again!

Speaking: looking back

Look back through Units 13 and 14.

1. Find one photo you like. Say why you like it.
2. Which activity did you enjoy the most? Say why you liked it and what you learned from doing it.

Reading: a quiz

1. **Work in pairs. Find the answers to these questions in Units 13 and 14.**
   1. Which is the biggest country that the River Nile flows through?
   2. Where did Anton's journey end?
   3. Who was the ancient Egyptian god of the River Nile?
   4. When was the first Extreme Ironing World Championships?
   5. What do you need to do soap carving?

2. **Write five more questions to ask about Units 13 and 14.**

3. **Work with another pair. Ask and answer your questions.**

Listening: a bridge

1. **Read the sentences about the Ponte Vecchio bridge. Can you put them in the correct order?**

   a. It was built in 1345, but a few hundred years later a new part was built along the top.

   b. I think it would be cool to live and work on a bridge!

   c. It's very old; in fact, its name means 'old bridge' in English.

   d. When I was on holiday last year, I was walking with my parents when we saw an amazing bridge.

   e. There are lots of little houses and shops on it. The shops are still open every day to sell to the tourists.

   f. It's quite long because the river is wide, but what I liked is that people have lived on it since it was built.

2. 🔊 **Listen to check the correct order.**

Use of English: what are they?

1 Work in pairs. Choose six words from the box.

| crocodile | customer | editor | enemy | ferry | gorilla | hippo | hobby |
| lawyer | nutrient | pharmacy | pyramid | reward | soldier | traffic | turtle |

Write a sentence to explain each word, following these instructions.
- Start your sentences like this:

    Someone who …   *An animal which …*   *Something that …*

- Write your six sentences on a piece of paper.
- Don't write the words you have chosen.

2 Exchange sentences with another pair. Read your new sentences and work out the words.

Use of English: what I had done by the time I was 10

1 How much do you remember about your life before you were **10** years old? What were the most exciting and interesting things you remember?

2 Tell a partner.

By the time I was 10, I had | seen …
visited …
been to …
eaten …
met …
…

Did you know…?
Some adults in England were asked what they remembered before they were 10 years old. Seventy-three percent said that they had been to the beach with their family.

3 Write five of your sentences.

Vocabulary: *countdown*

What's the longest word you can make out of these letters?

Writing: a journey

Imagine that you went on the journey you planned in the Project on page **152**. Write an email to a friend to tell him / her about it.

Write about:

- a where you went
- b what you saw and did
- c what you enjoyed the most
- d what you learned from making the journey.

Space travel 15

Looking forward

This unit explores the history of space travel and how people live and work on the International Space Station.

You will read
- about life on the International Space Station (ISS)
- about gravity and how to calculate weight on other planets

You will listen
- to a talk about the key points in the history of space travel
- to astronauts talking about life on the ISS, as part of a project

You will speak
- about the history of space travel
- in a group debate about jobs

You will write
- to give reasons and arguments
- an email about life on the ISS, as part of a project

You will learn
- about adverbs, their position and their order
- about adjectives followed by prepositions
- about some multi-word verbs
- about the present passive

Blast off!

Listening: setting the scene

Discuss.

- What do these compound nouns mean? Match them to the photos on pages 165 and 166.

  spacecraft   space shuttle   space station

- These words are used in the talk about space travel which you are going to listen to. What do they mean? Use a dictionary, if necessary.

  astronaut   Earth   orbit (verb)   land (verb)

- What do you know about the history of space travel?

Listening: specific facts and information

1. Look at the infographic about the history of space travel. Can you complete the missing information?

2. 🔊 *The first travellers in space were animals.* Listen to the first part of the talk and complete the information in 1–4.

3. Listen to the second part of the talk and complete the information in 5–7.

4. Listen to the whole of the talk. Complete the years a–f.

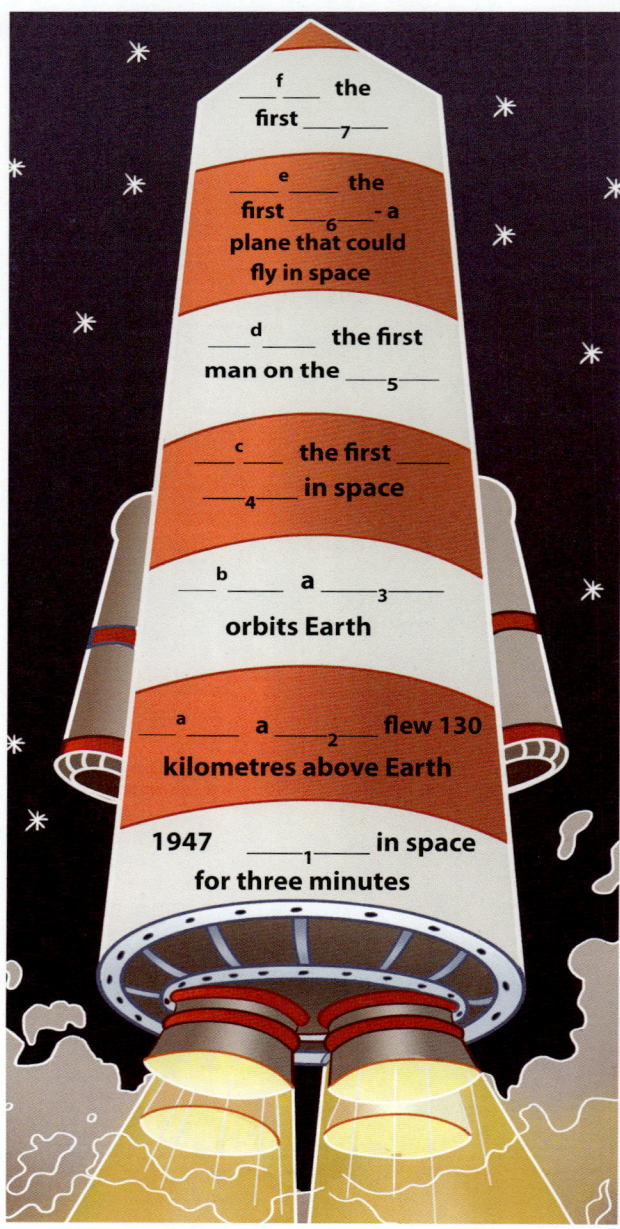

___f___ the first ___7___

___e___ the first ___6___ - a plane that could fly in space

___d___ the first man on the ___5___

___c___ the first ___ ___4___ in space

___b___ a ___3___ orbits Earth

___a___ a ___2___ flew 130 kilometres above Earth

1947 ___1___ in space for three minutes

listen for main points and specific information

Use of English: adverbs and their position

1 **Look at these sentences from the talk.**

They returned <u>safely</u> <u>to Earth</u>.

The first man went <u>into space</u> <u>in 1961</u>.

A space station <u>never</u> returns <u>to Earth</u>.

It will <u>probably</u> be used <u>until 2024</u>.

1 Which part of speech are the underlined words?
2 Adverbs tell us about *how, where, when, how often* and *how certain*. Find one example of each type of adverb in the sentences above.

2 **Look at the position of the adverbs in the sentences above.**

1 Are most of them at the beginning, in the middle or at the end of the sentence?
2 Which adverbs have a different position?
3 Can any of the adverbs move to a different position in the sentence?

3 **The first two sentences in activity 1 above and the three sentences in 4 below have more than one adverb (or adverb phrase). What is the order for *how*, *when* and *where* adverbs?**

A rocket takes off *slowly* *at first*.

Astronauts have to work *hard* *on a space station*.

Neil Armstrong ran and jumped *on the Moon* *for two and a half hours*.

4 **Work in pairs. Reorder to make sentences.**

1 walked / in 1969 / on the Moon / a man /
2 certainly / will / see / next week / I / you /
3 usually / on Saturdays / at home / we are /

Use of English: adjective + preposition

Work in pairs. Make sentences with these pairs of words.

> excited about   famous for   good at
> frightened of   kind to   tired of

> I'm excited about seeing the International Space Station when it next passes over my area.

Language tip

Some adjectives are followed by a preposition (for example, *tired of*). Using a different preposition sometimes changes the meaning (for example, *angry* **with** [someone] or *angry* **about** [something]).

There are no rules about which preposition to use, so you have to learn them. You can make a list in your notebook and add each new adjective + preposition you learn.

pre-verbal, post-verbal and end-position adverbs; adjectives with dependent prepositions

The International Space Station (ISS)

Reading: setting the scene

Discuss.

- What do you know about the International Space Station (ISS)?
- What do you think it's like to live on the ISS? Where and how do you think astronauts:
  - sleep
  - eat
  - relax?
- Read the text to see if you were right about life on the ISS.

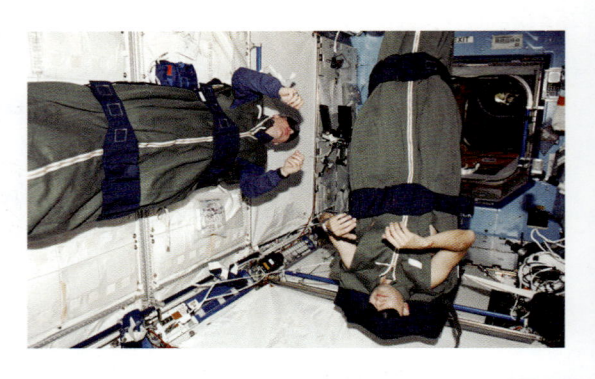

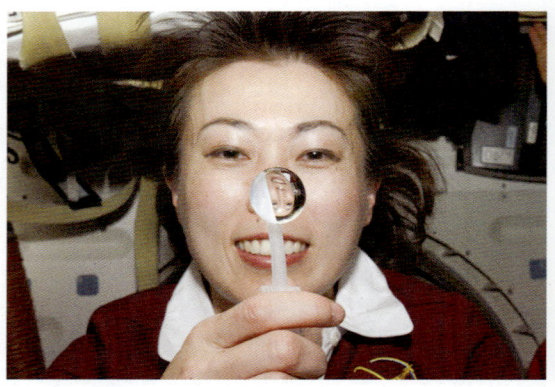

Have you ever thought about what it's like to live in space? Well, six astronauts on the ISS are doing that right now.

The ISS flies 400 kilometres above our heads at a speed of eight kilometres per second. It orbits Earth once every 90 minutes. That means the crew see the Sun rise and set 16 times in a day! However, they try to live a normal life. They sleep, eat, work and relax just as we do. But some things are a bit different!

There is no gravity on the ISS, so nothing falls down, it floats around. When the astronauts sleep, they tie themselves to a wall in their small bedrooms. It doesn't matter which wall, it can even be the floor or the ceiling, because there is no up or down.

The astronauts' day starts when the lights are turned on. They get up at six o'clock – but perhaps 'get up' is the wrong verb, when there is no up! They brush their teeth just like we do. The toothpaste is easy, because it sticks to the toothbrush, but water can be more of a problem. It forms into big balls and floats around, so the astronauts have to catch it with their mouths!

The space station must be clean and safe, just like your home. So, after breakfast, the astronauts have to clean the space station and then get to work. Most of them are scientists, so they have experiments to work on.

In the evening, the astronauts relax. They can email or call their families. Most of them say they never get tired of watching Earth pass by their windows, because they can enjoy views that the rest of us will never see.

read for main points

Reading: understanding the text

1. In what ways are the lives of astronauts on the ISS similar to our lives?

2. In what ways are the lives of the astronauts different from our lives?

3. Why did the author write this text?
   a To teach scientists about the ISS.
   b To interest and excite readers.
   c To get people to give money for the ISS.

4. Which do you think is the best title for the text?
   a The International Space Station
   b Astronauts
   c A daily routine like no other!

> **Did you know …?**
> You can see the ISS yourself. It is the third brightest object in the night sky. The light looks like a plane, but it moves much faster. To learn when and where to watch out for the ISS in your area, search on the internet for 'Spot the station NASA'.

Vocabulary: words in context

1. Match the words from the text with their meanings.

   > crew   rise   set   gravity   float
   > tie   stick   experiment

   a a scientific test to find out what happens when something is done to someone / something
   b the force that makes something fall to the ground
   c the people who work together, usually on a ship or plane
   d to move down in the sky, at the end of the day
   e to move up in the sky, at the beginning of the day
   f to stay in position because it is joined in some way
   g to stay in the air
   h to use something (for example, a rope) to make something or somebody stay in place

2. *Bedroom* is a one-word compound noun. Can you find two others in the text?

read to understand detail and deduce meaning, and to recognise purpose

Vocabulary: multi-word verbs

Match these verbs with their meanings.

1	get away	a	arrive at a place and time
2	get back	b	be better after an illness
3	get in	c	be friends with someone
4	get on	d	be given something you had before
5	get over	e	escape
6	get together	f	meet

Use of English: the present passive

> **Language tip**
>
> The author says *'get up' is the wrong verb when there is no up!* So, what can we say when astronauts leave their beds? Is 'get down', 'get over', 'get through' or 'get about' better?
>
> There are a lot of verbs that include 'get' and another word. We call these multi-word verbs.

1 Look at this sentence from the text and answer the questions.

The astronauts' day starts when the lights are turned on.

1. Do the astronauts turn on the lights?
2. Is it important for the reader to know who turns on the lights?
3. Why did the writer use a passive verb tense?
4. On page 32 we looked at how to form the past simple passive. How do we form the present simple passive?

2 Work in pairs. Make sentences using these words and phrases.

a astronauts / teach / how to live without gravity

> Astronauts are taught how to live without gravity.

b the space station / clean / before the astronauts start work
c science experiments / do / on the ISS
d in Thailand / soap / carve / to make beautiful flowers
e the carvings / sell / to tourists

170 prepositional verbs; present simple passive

Who wants to be an astronaut?

Speaking: a balloon debate

1 Work in groups. Discuss.
- Would you like to be an astronaut? Why / Why not?
- Would you like to have one of the jobs in the word cloud? Make sure you understand what each of the jobs is. Choose one job that everyone in your group would like.

filmmaker, hairdresser, vet, astronaut, detective, builder, scientist, firefighter, athlete, politician

2 Listen while your teacher tells a story about a class trip which goes wrong. Then discuss what to do.

Writing: giving reasons and arguments

You are going to write a formal report about your discussion.

- Explain why you and your job will be useful on the island. Give as many reasons as possible. Start:

  I am a … When we arrive on the island, I will be extremely useful because …

- Say which job you think will not be useful on the island. Give three reasons. Start:

  For the following reasons, I believe a … will not be useful on the island. First, …

Some other useful phrases

I believe that …   It is clear that …   I think you will agree that …

My second point is …   Finally, …   To conclude, …

speak using appropriate register, to give and respond to opinions

Focus on Maths

Calculating our weight on other planets

1 Before you read, discuss what you know about gravity. Answer these questions.
- What does gravity do?
- What happens when there is no gravity, for example, in space?
- Is gravity the same on all planets?

We all know that if we let go of something heavy, it will fall. This is because gravity pulls everything towards the centre of Earth. However, gravity is more important than this. It is what holds everything on Earth together. It is what stops us from falling off Earth and flying out into space. Gravity is the reason why rocks and seas are able to hold together to make planets, moons and stars. It is the reason why planets orbit stars (in the way that Earth orbits our star, the Sun). Gravity is also the reason why the stars stay together in huge groups.

Astronauts on a space station feel weightless because there is no gravity. If they go outside for a space walk, they must tie themselves onto something or else they will float away. When astronauts went to the Moon, they were not weightless. This was because there is some gravity on the Moon, but not much. They found that they could jump very easily – around six times higher and further than they could on Earth – but gravity still brought them back to the ground.

So, if we go to the Moon or to a space station for a visit, do our bodies change? Does it change again when we get back to Earth? Of course not, our bodies stay the same! We can say that our *mass remains constant*, but that, because of gravity, we can feel more or less heavy. We can calculate our weight on a planet by multiplying our mass by the gravity on that planet.

weight = mass × gravity

Look at the graph and Table 1 on page 173. They show the gravity on different planets when compared with Earth. The gravity on Earth is given as 1.0.

Planet / moon	Gravity relative to Earth
Sun	27.9
Mercury	0.38
Venus	0.91
Earth	1.0
Moon	0.17
Mars	0.38
Jupiter	2.54
Saturn	1.08
Uranus	0.91
Neptune	1.19

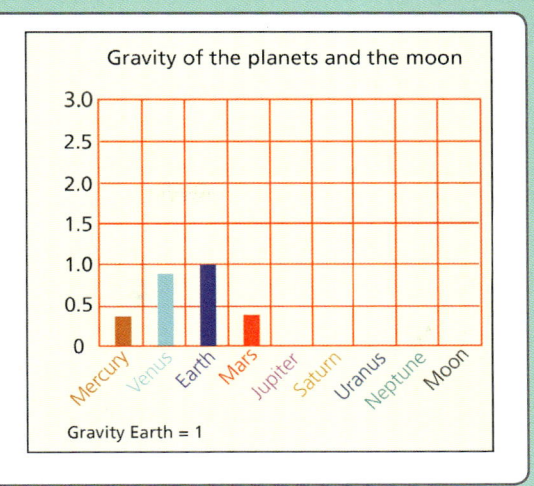

Table 1

2 Copy and complete the graph. Use the information in the table.

3 Work in pairs. Answer the questions.

1 Which planets have more gravity than Earth?
2 Which two planets have the least gravity?
3 Jupiter is the biggest planet and Mercury is the smallest planet. Why do you think the Moon might have less gravity than any of the planets?
4 Why can't you draw a bar for the Sun on this graph?

4 Once you know the gravity on each planet when compared with Earth, you can work out how heavy you will feel there. Copy and complete Table 2.

- Find out your weight in kilograms. Write it in the top row of Table 2.
- Multiply your Earth weight by the relative gravity figures for each planet in Table 1 above, to find your weight. For example, if you weigh 50 kg on Earth, you can calculate that you will weigh 19 kg on Mercury.

  50 × 0.38 = 19

Planet / moon	My weight
Earth	
Mercury	
Venus	
Mars	
Jupiter	
Saturn	
Uranus	
Neptune	
Moon	
Sun	

Table 2

5 Match the words from the text with their meanings.

1 weightless
2 calculate
3 mass
4 remain
5 constant
6 multiply
7 compared with

a continuing the same
b having no weight
c looking at ways in which two things are similar or different
d the amount of matter that something has
e to get a number by adding another number to itself a number of times
f to stay and not to change
g to work out a number or amount by using maths

understand and use main points

Project: life on the ISS

In this project you are going to research life on the ISS and write an email.

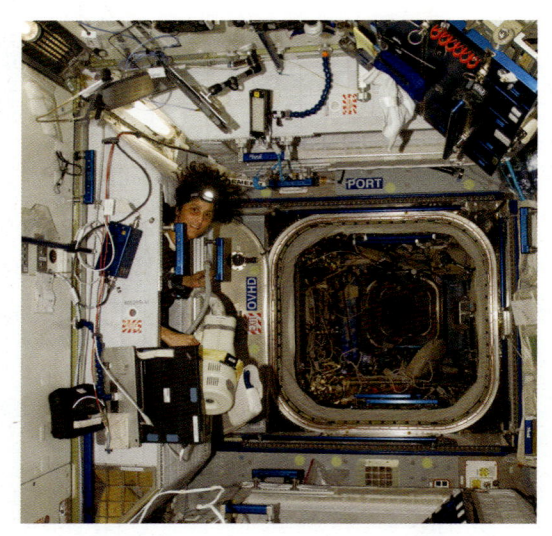

1 Imagine that you are an astronaut living on the ISS and that you receive this email.

To: astronaut@iss.nasa.gov
From: scienceclass@earthscool.com
Subject: Life on the ISS
Hi! My class saw a picture of you on the ISS. You have such an amazing life! Can you tell us more about it? What do you do all day? What do you like to eat? Do you get to talk to your family? Do you have a TV? We have so many questions. Please tell us what you can. Mr Henderson's Year 7 Science class, Earth

2 Research information about what life is like on the ISS.

You can find a lot of information on the NASA website (NASA is the organisation that controls the ISS). Ask your teacher to help you find it online.

The website includes some very interesting videos of astronauts talking about life on the ISS. As you listen and watch, make notes about some of the interesting things you learn.

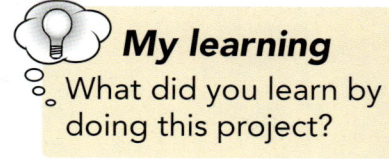

My learning
What did you learn by doing this project?

3 Write a reply to the email, as if you are an astronaut. Tell the Year 7 children some exciting and interesting facts about life on the ISS.

use reference resources; understand specific information in extended narrative

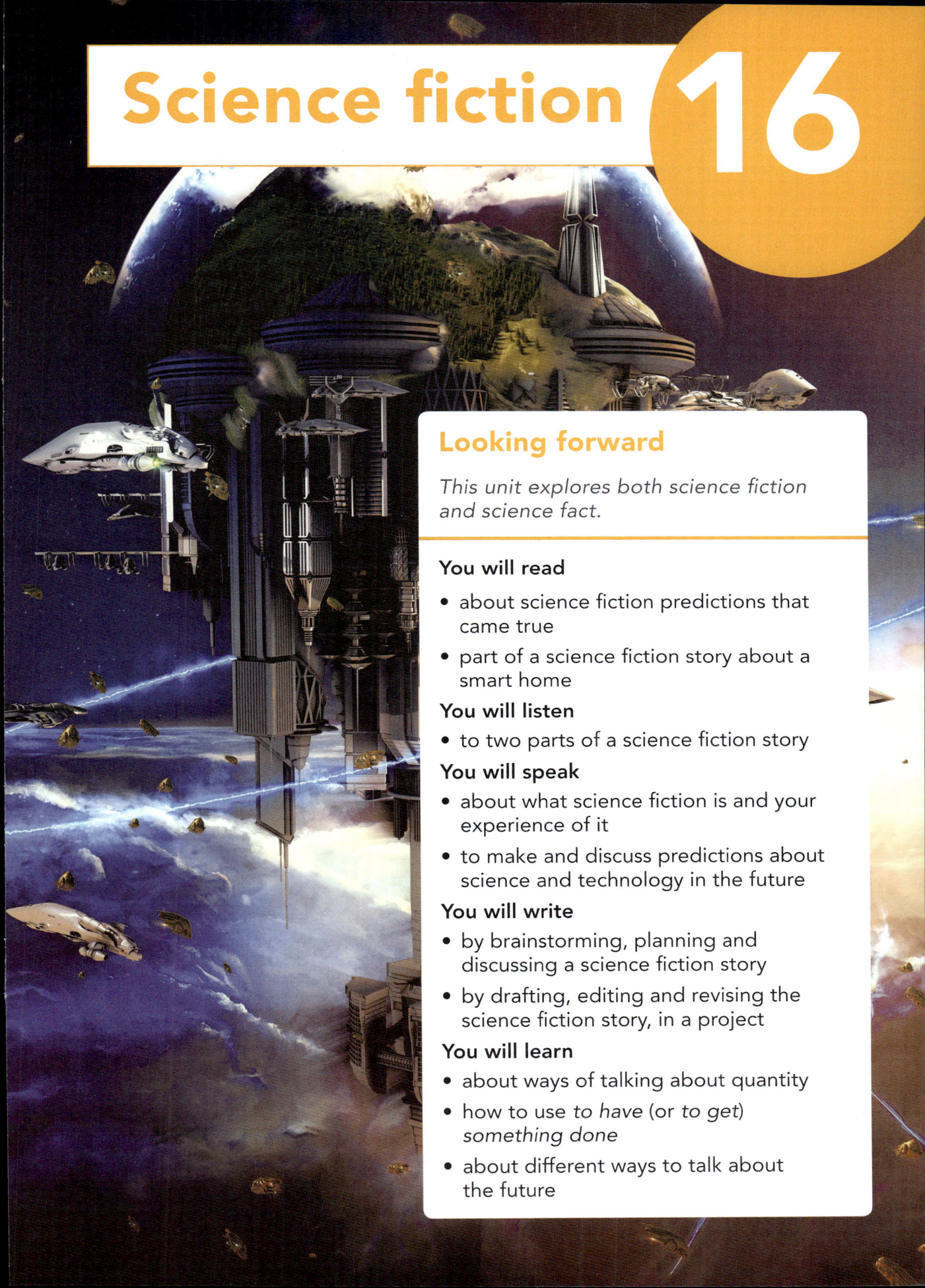

Science fiction 16

Looking forward

This unit explores both science fiction and science fact.

You will read
- about science fiction predictions that came true
- part of a science fiction story about a smart home

You will listen
- to two parts of a science fiction story

You will speak
- about what science fiction is and your experience of it
- to make and discuss predictions about science and technology in the future

You will write
- by brainstorming, planning and discussing a science fiction story
- by drafting, editing and revising the science fiction story, in a project

You will learn
- about ways of talking about quantity
- how to use *to have* (or *to get*) *something done*
- about different ways to talk about the future

Science fiction or science fact?

Speaking: what is science fiction?

Discuss.

- What is science fiction? How is it different from other types of fiction (for example, crime, adventure, horror)?
- Which of these sentences describes science fiction?
    - It is about a crime, what happens as a result of the crime, and how the crime is solved.
    - It is about strange and magical things, with unreal settings and characters.
    - It is about unreal things that could be real in the future, in our world or in a different world.
    - It is about friendship, love and problems between people.
- What science fiction stories or films do you know? What happens in them?

Reading: exploring the text

Read the language tip. Then look at the text quickly. Don't read every word.

Is the text about:

a predictions that science fiction stories written in the present make about the future

b predictions made by science fiction stories written in the past, which have come true in the present?

> **Language tip**
> When we *predict* the future, we say what we think will happen. Science fiction is full of *predictions* about the future.

A lot of the interest created in a science fiction story is the picture it paints of the future. Will there be flying cars? Will we live on other planets? Will there be homes under the sea?

Some science fiction stories that were written in the past did extremely well at predicting the future. Here are three ideas from science fiction that became science fact.

1 In 1865 science fiction writer Jules Verne predicted the first journey to the Moon. He wrote about a spacecraft blasting off from Florida in the USA and then returning and landing in the sea. All of this actually happened over a hundred years later, in 1969.

2 *In the Year 2889* is a science fiction story written in 1889, also by Jules Verne, which describes a machine called a **phonotelephote**. People who used the machine could see and talk to each other when they were many kilometres apart. We didn't have to wait until 2889 for this machine, because in 1964 the world saw its first real 'picturephone', and today Skype and FaceTime have become common ways to communicate.

read for main points

3 This is one I can't wait to try! If you've seen any of the *Star Wars* films made since 1983, you will have seen people driving hoverbikes, which are flying motorbikes. Real hoverbikes have now been invented, and since 2017 they have been available for people to buy. They are able to carry two people and can fly into small places that a helicopter can't get into.

It seems that science fiction does become true – so, what's next?

Reading: understanding the text

Read the text and answer the questions.
1. What does the author say is an important part of science fiction?
2. How many years were there between Jules Verne's prediction and the first time a *picturephone* was used?
3. Why are *Skype* and *FaceTime* mentioned in the text?
4. What do you think hoverbikes will be used for?
5. Think of a title for the text. The title should be about the text. It should be interesting so that a reader will want to read it.

Vocabulary: words in context

Find these words in the text and match them to their meanings.

| interest | apart | common | invented | available |

a at a distance from something else
b can be used, taken or bought
c happening a lot
d made or created something new
e what something has to make you notice it and want to know more about it

Use of English: quantity

1 Look at these sentences from the text.

A lot of the interest in a science fiction story …

All of this happened over a hundred years later …

The underlined words add information to the sentence. What kind of information is it?

2 Make sentences using the phrases below.

both of the books   half the size
twice the price   all this time

> Both of the books in the text are by Jules Verne.

read for specific information and deduce meaning; determiners

What's next?

Listening: setting the scene

1 Check that you know the meaning of these words. Use a dictionary, if necessary.

professor   robot   task   complicated   database   knowledge

2 All the words are in the passage you are going to listen to. Can you predict what it will be about?

Listening: a story

1 🔊 Read the questions. Then listen to find the answers.
1 Who is talking?
2 What are they talking about?
   a cooking
   b how robots have got better
   c why robots don't work

2 Listen again. Discuss answers to these questions.
1 Why does the professor talk about boiling an egg?
2 As an example of cooking, is boiling an egg simple or complicated?
3 As an example of what people have to do, is boiling an egg simple or complicated?
4 Gavin gives an example of when he was little. Is he agreeing or disagreeing with the professor?
5 Can robots boil eggs at the time the professor is talking?
6 What does the professor want robots to be able to do in the future?

Use of English: *to have / get something done*

1 Which do you think is more important for the professor?
   a to know how to boil an egg himself
   b to know how to have an egg boiled by a robot

2 Look at these sentences. What is the difference in meaning between the A and B sentences?

A I cut my hair.	B I had my hair cut.
A She took a photo of herself.	B She had a photo taken of herself.
A My dad washed his car.	B My dad got his car washed.

listen for main points, specific information and implied meaning

3 Complete this rule.

When we talk about something we have asked or paid someone else to do for us, we use the verbs ¹_____ or ²_____ + noun / pronoun + ³_____ participle.

4 Work in pairs. Look carefully at the word order of these sentences. Discuss.

What's the difference between these sentences? How could you complete them?

A Gavin had an egg boiled …   B Gavin had boiled an egg …

5 Imagine that you have a robot at home that does everything for you. Make sentences about what the robot did before you came to school this morning. Use *had* or *got*.

shower / turn on

breakfast / make

teeth / clean

hair / comb

bedroom / tidy

schoolbag / pack

> I had the shower turned on.

> But now I'm at school and I must do the work myself!

Speaking: making predictions

Work in groups. Discuss.

- Read what the professor said in the text:

  'But the dream has always been to build a robot that could learn, and therefore think, for itself.'

  Do you think this will happen? Do you think it would be a good thing?

- Read the last sentence of the text:

  It seems that science fiction does become true – so, what's next?

- Think about ideas have you seen or read about in science fiction stories. Do you think they will become science fact?

- Agree about three predictions for technology in the future. Tell the rest of the class.

causative forms; give opinions   179

Talking about the future

Use of English: four ways to talk about the future

1 When you were making predictions, which of these verb forms did you use the most?

   a present simple tense   b present continuous tense
   c *will* + verb   d *be going to* + verb

2 Are these sentences about the present or future? Which verb tenses do they use?

   1 On Monday I'm watching the new *Star Trek* film with Abel.
   2 What time are you leaving tomorrow?
   3 The film starts at 07:30.
   4 When does it finish?

3 Can you think of any other examples of the present continuous and present simple used to talk about the future?

4 Copy and complete this timetable. Plan what you are going to do at the weekend.

day	_____	_____
07:00–10:00		
10:00–13:00		
13:00–16:00		
16:00–19:00		
19:00–22:00		

> **Language tip**
> There are four different ways we can talk about the future – all of the ways given in activity 1 above.

> **Did you know …?**
> Nikola Tesla predicted wi-fi and mobile phones in 1909.

- Write activities in six of the boxes. Leave four of the boxes empty.
- Work in pairs. Make arrangements to meet. Don't look at each other's timetables.

> What are you doing on Saturday evening?

> I'm visiting my cousins.

> Are you free on Saturday morning after 10?

> Sure, I'm free. What are we going to do?

Writing: planning a story

You are going to work in groups to plan a science fiction story.

1. Read this information about science fiction stories.

> **Writing a science fiction story**
>
> A science fiction story will often include the following:
>
> *Setting:* In the future, on a spacecraft or on another planet.
>
> *Characters:* Two or three humans on a journey through space. Some strange people or creatures from other planets.
>
> *Plot:* The main characters will face problems and dangers on their journey. These will be solved, often as a result of science or technology.
>
> *Other:* Machines and technology that we don't have now. Some scientific words (that can be made up) and descriptions.

2. Discuss the ideas that you would like to put in your story. Think about the predictions you made during the **Speaking: making predictions** activity on page 179.
3. Copy and complete a plan for your story.

Setting	
Characters	
Plot	
Other	

4. Compare your plan with those of other groups.
   - Read the other plans. Ask the groups questions about their story plans.
   - Answer questions about your own story plan.
5. Revise your story plan. You will write the story during the project lesson.

My learning

We learn by doing and then by thinking about what we have done.

Think about the plan you wrote and what your friends said about it.

How could you make it better?

brainstorm and plan written work 181

Focus on Literature

Eager

The listening passage about Gavin and the professor came from a science fiction story called *Eager*. You are now going to read part of this story. In it, Gavin Bell and his family live in a smart house that does everything for them. It listens to instructions and can talk.

1 What do you know about *smart homes*?

2 🔊 Listen to this passage from *Eager*. Don't read anything yet. Then answer these questions.

   1 Who are the main characters?   2 Where does the story take place?
   3 What time of day is it?   4 Is Gavin happy?

> **Reading tip**
>
> A text may have a lot of words you don't know, but it's not necessary to know every word to understand or to enjoy reading. In this case, some words are explained in *Word help*, and you can work out the meaning of others.

3 Read and check your answers.

The hours passed and the house grew busier – waking everyone up and setting the temperature for showers and baths. It checked the gobetween for news that might interest the Bells, adjusted roof panels to create more heat, and raised the blinds on the day ahead.

Gavin was the first to come downstairs. He was in a bad mood, though he didn't know why. He had been looking forward to today. After home study he was going to the learning centre for a game of liveball. That was the good bit. On the other hand, he was sure he had instructed the house to wake him with his favourite music; instead, a shrill voice had screeched 'wakey! wakey!' in his ear.

'Where is everyone?'

Word help

setting – making a machine ready to work
adjust – to change or move something so that it works or fits better
roof panels – flat pieces on a roof which collect solar power
blinds – a type of curtain that goes up and down over a window
a shrill voice had screeched 'wakey! wakey!' – a horrible high voice shouted 'wake up!'
nappy – a soft piece of cloth or paper that a baby wears
soothing – gentle and calm
snapped – spoke in a sudden and angry way
prompted – helped or encouraged to say something
flicker – to go on and off quickly
stubborn and sulky – difficult, unhelpful and unhappy

'Your mother is in the shower and your father is changing Charlotte's nappy,' replied the house in a soothing, feminine voice. 'Your sister is …'

'All right,' snapped Gavin. 'I didn't really expect an answer. It was a rit … ret …'

'Rhetorical question?' prompted the house.

'Yes, I know.' Gavin sat down to adjust his sock. 'Anyway, you're not supposed to be on in here. You know Mum doesn't like machines in the dining room.'

'I am not a machine,' corrected the house.

'Yes you are, drybrain. You just don't have a body.' He looked up. 'Go on then, turn yourself off.'

There was a long pause before the green light beside the door began to flicker, and an even longer pause before it went out. Gavin frowned. He knew that machines were not supposed to have personalities, apart from the one people might choose for them. But if anyone had asked him, he would have said that the house was stubborn and sulky.

from **Eager** *by Helen Fox*

4 You can work out some new words just looking at them.
1 What do you think *liveball* is?
2 What about *feminine*? Does it mean *like a man* or *like a woman*?

5 Other new words you can work out by looking at the context (the words and sentences around them). Find these words in the text and decide on their meaning.
1 *gobetween* is a word that has been made up for this story – do you think it is:
 a something that brings news into the house
 b someone who brings the newspaper?
2 What about a *rhetorical* question? Is it one that:
 a doesn't need an answer b needs a long answer?
3 *drybrain* is another word that has been made up for the story – do you think Gavin says this name:
 a to be kind because he is happy b to be unkind because he is angry?

Work in pairs. Find the words in the text and discuss their meaning. Use a dictionary to check your answers.

mood   voice   expect   pause   frowned   personality

6 Work in groups. Discuss.
1 What in the text suggests that there is something wrong with the house?
2 What do you think will happen in this story?

read for main points and deduce meaning

Project: a science fiction story

In this project you are going to work in groups to write your science fiction story.

> **Story tips**
> - A story must have beginning, a middle and an end.
> - The characters should face problems, which they solve. This is the adventure which makes the story exciting and interesting.

1 Copy and complete this table to plan your story from Writing on page 181 in more detail.

Title	
Beginning	
Build-up	
Problems	
How solved	
End	

2 Work together as a group to write your story. Choose how you are going to do this.

- One can write as others tell the story.
- Each one of you can write a different part of the story.
- Each of you can write your own story based on the story plan.

3 Edit the story. To be a good writer, you must always check and revise what you write.

> **Editing tips**
> - Read your story carefully. Look for mistakes and for ways in which you can make it better.
> - Make changes or, better still, write it again.

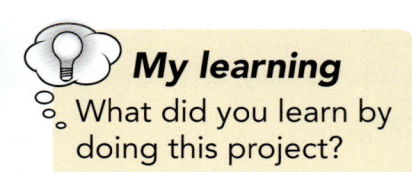

My learning
What did you learn by doing this project?

4 Revise or rewrite your story. Make it ready to show others.

End-of-year review

Vocabulary: *Blockbusters*

Listen to your teacher and play *Blockbusters*.

Writing: *Blockbusters clues*

Work in pairs. Prepare to play *Blockbusters*.
Think of a word for each of the letters in the grid.
Then think of a clue (not a question) for each word.
Write the clues and the answers on a piece of paper.

   m: *something that is not correct (mistake)*

Speaking: play *Blockbusters*

1. Copy the *Blockbusters* grid.

2. Work in groups of four. Play the game.
   - The first pair reads out their clues. The second pair plays against each other using the grid.
   - Change roles.

Use of English: multi-word verbs

1. Work in pairs. Your teacher will give you one of these four lists of multi-word verbs. Write a sentence using each verb to show its meaning. Use a dictionary, if necessary.

A		B		C		D	
	turn off		turn down		turn on		turn up
	turn into		turn out		turn over		turn to
	get away		get back		get in		get on
	get over		get together		get off		look up
	break into		take away		put up		take off

2. Now work with another pair who wrote sentences for the same list. Compare your sentences. Decide which is the best example sentence for each verb.

3. Work in a new group of four (everyone will have looked at verbs from different lists). Take turns to explain the meaning of your verbs and to read out your example sentences.

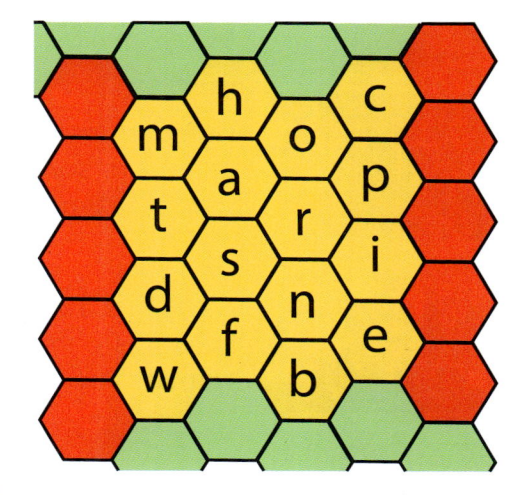

Reading: matching

Amy, Chico, Andy and Nina want to start a new hobby or sport. Read the descriptions of six hobbies and sports below the descriptions of each person. Choose the most suitable activity for each person.

	Amy wants to do something new and exciting. She loves adventure and is not afraid of danger. She goes swimming in an indoor pool every day, but she wants to do something outside at the weekends.
	Chico is creative and artistic. He wants to learn new skills so that he can make something he will be proud of. He thinks most sports are a waste of time because you haven't created anything when you finish.
	Andy has a very busy life. He studies hard at school, and he also helps his parents in their shop. He doesn't have much time, but he wants to do something that will help him relax and forget work.
	Nina wants to meet more people. She is very friendly and enjoys working in teams. She also thinks she is a bit overweight, so she wants to do more exercise.

Volleyball

Wouldn't you like to try a new sport that isn't expensive and isn't difficult, but will keep you fit and is great fun? Volleyball is played in teams of six players and needs just two teams, a net and a ball. It's an increasingly popular sport. It can be played indoors or outdoors, and is often played on the beach.

Birdwatching

What a wonderful way to spend a day with a group of friends – or quietly on your own. You'll need some binoculars to see the birds better, and a book to help you recognise them. The rest is up to you – you can sit and wait for the birds to come to you, or take long walks to find them. A great way to keep fit, relax and learn about nature at the same time.

Pottery

There's nothing quite like getting your hands dirty and producing something beautiful out of a lump of clay. You'll learn how to prepare the clay, use a potter's wheel to make the shapes, and then finish your pottery. At the end of the course, you'll be well on your way to making pots and vases for your friends and family.

Cross-country running

This is exactly what it says. You find a pair of trainers and start running! You can run on small country roads, on paths through fields or forests, or along a beach. It will keep you fit and healthy, but also being outside in nature on your own will help you to relax and forget your problems.

Yoga

This type of exercise comes from ancient Indian learning. It strengthens the body and the mind. An important part of yoga is learning how to breathe well. It all helps to produce a feeling of peace and quiet. You can learn in a class with a teacher, or study with our video programme. From the beginning, you'll be able to practise on your own, anywhere, at any time.

Kitesurfing

If you love the sea and have enjoyed surfing or waterskiing, then kitesurfing could be for you. You use a board, and catch the wind with a large kite. It's just you, the wind and the sea. With a little experience, you can get up to speeds of 100 kmh and make high jumps.

Use of English: rewording

For each question, complete the second sentence so that it means the same as the first.

1. a Climate change endangers some animals.
   b Some animals … climate change.
2. a Her hair was cut yesterday.
   b She … her hair … yesterday.
3. a Our animals are very good friends and they look after each other.
   b Our animals are … good friends … they look after each other.
4. a We were lucky because we bought an umbrella and then ten minutes later it started to rain.
   b It started to rain but luckily we … an umbrella ten minutes before.
5. a I go to the pool at six o'clock every morning because I love swimming.
   b I love swimming. … I go to the pool at six o'clock very morning.

Listening: conversations

Listen to the three conversations. Read these questions and choose the best answers.

1 What does the visitor do?

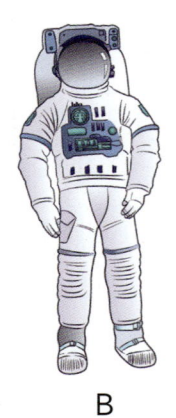

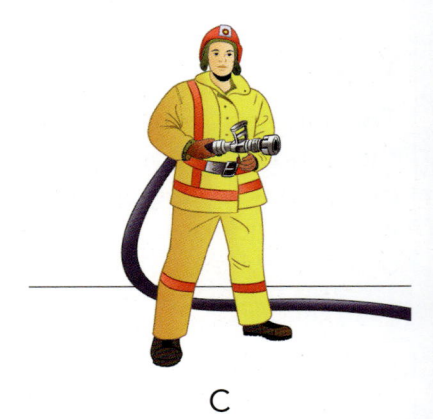

A   B   C

2 What hobby has the girl been doing?

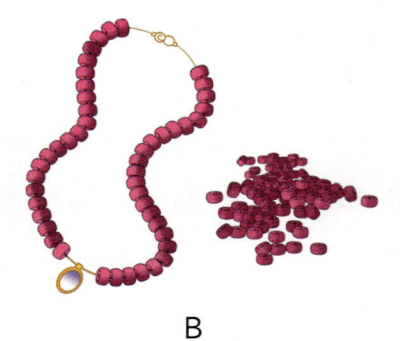

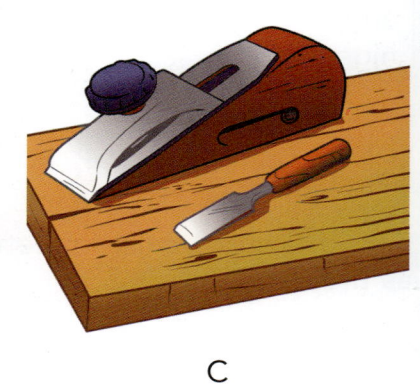

A   B   C

3 How did the boy travel to school?

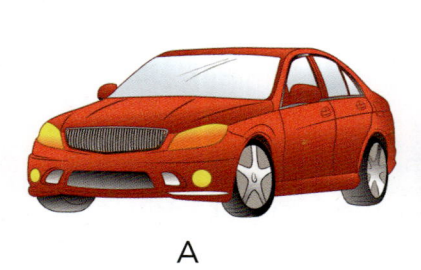

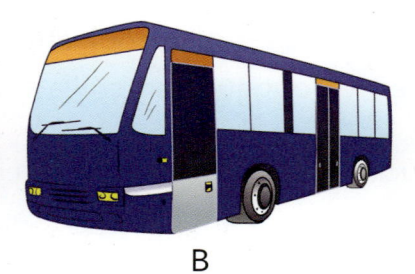

A   B   C

188 end-of-year review

Speaking: a balloon debate

Do you remember the balloon debate about jobs, in Unit **15**? You are going to have another debate, but this time it will be about famous people.

- Work in groups. Choose a famous person everyone knows a lot about. Make notes about what he or she has done.
- Imagine that your famous person is in the balloon with other groups of famous people. Tell the rest of the class why your famous person should stay in the balloon. Explain what he/she will do on the island.
- Discuss in your group which famous person you think should go out of the balloon. Then tell the rest of the class. If any group chooses your group's famous person, listen carefully to their reasons, and then disagree with them.

Use of English: correction competition

Work in pairs. Read the instructions for the competition.

- Read the sentences. Six are incorrect and two are correct.
- Win one mark for each incorrect sentence that you can find.
- Win two marks for each incorrect sentence that you can correct.
- The winner is the pair with the most points.

1. We mustn't to be late again.
2. Have you ever played *Blockbusters*?
3. The air temperature is now increasing more quick than in the past.
4. If it rained more often, there will be more water in the rivers and lakes.
5. I really don't enjoy to swim in cold water.
6. If we go now, they'll all be in home.
7. I had learned to read before I started school.
8. You have to work at school hard if you want to do well.

Vocabulary: words in context

1 Read these sentences about climate and climate change. Choose the best word to complete them.

1. After the storm, the water _____ into the rivers and lakes.
   - **a** polluted
   - **b** put
   - **c** poured
2. There was such a strong wind that it _____ down trees and turned over lorries.
   - **a** broke
   - **b** blew
   - **c** breathed

end-of-year review 189

3 When the temperature _____ around the world, it changes the whole climate.
   a rises   b replaces   c reuses

4 It saves energy and helps the environment if we can _____ things to give them another use.
   a reduce   b recycle   c relax

2 Read these sentences about wildlife. Choose the best word to complete them.

1 It is important to _____ the number of endangered animals and what is threatening them, in order to help save them.
   a rescue   b research   c reach

2 We need to _____ wild animals, or they will be gone and we will never see them again.
   a prepare   b produce   c protect

3 There has been a small _____ in the number of tigers.
   a increase   b interest   c inform

4 One threat to mountain gorillas is a _____ which they can catch from people.
   a defeat   b decrease   c disease

Writing: my report

1 Discuss.
- Have you enjoyed learning English this year?
- Do you think you have learned a lot?
- How well do you think you can: (a) speak; (b) listen; (c) read and; (d) write in English now?
- What do you still want to learn?

2 Write your own end-of-year report for English language. Write about:
- what you can do now
- what progress you have made
- what you need to work on next year.

You can give yourself a mark, if you like!

WELL DONE!

end-of-year review

Word list

UNIT 1
Africa
alphabet
Antarctica
Asia
Australia
billion
communicate
communication
continent
disgust
encyclopaedia
Europe
feeling
greet
greetings
look up
lorry
mother tongue
North America
opinion
pronunciation
recently
role
scream
search
section
sign
situation
South America

Focus on ICT
blog
followers
interact
microblog
mobile device
social media
social network
text
tweet

UNIT 2
advantage / disadvantage
bar (of soap/chocolate)
battery
change (noun)
checkout
choice
customer
department store
desktop (computer)
electronics
experience
huge
hypermarket
illness
jewellery
mini-market
newsagent
packet
pharmacy
plenty of
product
self-service
shop assistant
shopper
shopping mall
smartphone
specialist shop
store
toothpaste
traffic
tube
webcam

Focus on the World
float
floating
material
seller
stall
stick

UNIT 3
ancient
arrest
blurb
break into
celebrity
character
crime

criminal
detective
enemy
gun
hacker
headline
killing
law/lawyer
murderer
mystery
(police) officer
paragraph
pirate
plot
prison
report
reward
rob
robbery
setting
solve
steal
take away
thief
trial

Focus on Science
clue
compare
crime scene
data
evidence
examine

known
match
profile
puzzle
search
tears
tool

UNIT 4
bacteria
bite
candle
celebration
creature
decorate
deep
depth
design
dragon
escape
female
festival
firework
height
high
lay
length
live
long
male
monster
prepare

reptile
scare
scary
sharp
stick
weigh
weight
wide
width

Focus on Literature
cruel
folk tale
landowner
spade

UNIT 5
(rubbish) bin
basket
bin (verb)
collection
compare
comparison
description
display
exhibition
gallery
headline
memory
mistake
modern
pile
pottery

replace
response
rubbish
scene
sculpture
shape
smile
studio
textile

Focus on Art

abstract
ancient
cave
dimension
element
human form
jewellery
mask
natural
performance
subject
theme

UNIT 6

advert
aim (verb)
board
dive (verb)
diving
excitement
in common
interview

kite
kitesurfing
manager
mountain biking
outdoor
parachute
pour
put up
raft
relax
reporter
rock
rock climbing
rule (noun)
sailing
shoot
skateboarding
skiing
skydiving
snowboarding
speed
surf
surfing
waterskiing
wave
white-water rafting
windsurfing

Focus on the World

breath
breathe
calf
culture

fight
for instance
goat
grab
nation
touch
traditional

UNIT 7

arrival
battery
burn
camel
canoe
confusing
connect
continue
engine
environment
environmentally friendly
ferry
fuel
graphic
helicopter
human
lorry (or truck)
mix (noun)
plug in
pollute
pollution
power
produce

Word list 193

rail
reason
reduce
result
similar
solar
tram
transport
van
vehicle

Focus on Geography
cause
congestion
pedestrian
population
rural
solution
solve
traffic jam
traffic management
urban
urbanisation
zone

UNIT 8
action
adventure
amazing
amusing
annoyed
challenge
character
create

crime
drop
element
events
fiction
frightening
horror
humour
ingredients
non-fiction
overcome
perfect
plot
pot
rescue
romance
science fiction
setting
smell
stir
structure
tasty
theme
thick
traveller
treasure

Focus on Literature
poem
poetry
poet
rhyme
syllable
verse

UNIT 9
danger
disease
endangered
gorilla
gun
hunt
increase
intelligent
land
leader
local
net
ocean
officer
programme
protect
research
result
scientist
shoot
skin
successful
support
threat
tiger
tourism
turtle
unknown
wildlife

Focus on Science
amphibian

backbone
beak
classify
cold-blooded
feather
feed
fin
gill
invertebrate
lungs
mammal
reptile
scale
species
vertebrate
warm-blooded

UNIT 10
author
average
blow
climate
climate change
crops
decrease
depend on
disappear
Earth
edit
editor
glacier
global warming
graph

issue
malaria
melt
North / South Pole
pour
president
publish
recycle
reduce
reuse
rise
seem
tiny

Focus on the World
Canada
Central America
cyclone
equator
flood
ground
hurricane
India
Indian Ocean
monsoon
North America
Pacific Ocean
serious
spin
tornado
typhoon
USA
wave

UNIT 11
balance
balanced
cabbage
confused
confusing
diet
energy
experience
expert
fat (noun)
gain
gym
happiness
healthcare
illness
lecture
lifestyle
medicine
nutrient
overweight
put on
sugary
surprised
surprising
take off
tip
training
underweight

Focus on Health Science
carbohydrate
cereal

contain
fibre
mineral
properly
protein
repair
store
vitamin

UNIT 12
army
audience
cough
have nothing to do with
millionaire
notice
point
quiz
reach
series
silly
soldier
speed
successful
wish

Focus on Literature
brain
handcuffs
lucky
waiter

UNIT 13
complain
crocodile
destroy
extremely
flow
fly (noun)
go by
guide book
hippo
look forward to
mix
mosquito
nail
narrow
peace and quiet
pyramid
relax
source (of a river)
[+ names of countries and rivers]

Focus on History
agriculture
civilisation
dam
fertile
flood
god
goddess
kingdom

mud
nations
sail
sandals
soil
tomb
trade
unite

UNIT 14
attitude
carve
carving
championship
creative
design
detail
dust
encourage
extraordinary
hobby
invent
iron
ironing
long-haired
mobile
outline
persuade
rough
rub

serious
sewing
shape
skill
smart
smooth
squash
stamp collecting
step
underwater
yoga

Focus on the World
bone
control
develop
metal
recycle
wire

UNIT 15
[names of the 8 planets]
astronaut
athlete
builder
crew
Earth
experiment
filmmaker
firefighter

float
get away
get back
get in
get on
get over
get together
gravity
hairdresser
land (verb)
set
space
space shuttle
space station
orbit
politician
rise
spacecraft
stick
tie
vet

Focus on Maths
calculate
compared with
constant
graph
mass
multiply

planet
remain
weightless

UNIT 16
apart
available
boil
common
complicated
database
dream
interest
invent
knowledge
predict
prediction
professor
robot
task

Focus on Literature
expect
feminine
frown
mood
pause
personality
voice

Acknowledgements

The publishers wish to thank the following for permission to reproduce photographs. Every effort has been made to trace copyright holders and to obtain their permission for the use of copyright materials. The publishers will gladly receive any information enabling them to rectify any error or omission at the first opportunity.

Key: t = top, b = bottom, l = left, r = right, c = centre.

p7 Cienpies Design/Shutterstock, p8tr Creativa Images/Shutterstock, p8cl Evannovostro/Shutterstock, p8cr Filipe Frazao/Shutterstock, p8bl kostudio/Shutterstock, p8br Happy Together/Shutterstock, p9cl Evannovostro/Shutterstock, p9cr Filipe Frazao/Shutterstock, p9bl kostudio/Shutterstock, p9br Happy Together/Shutterstock, p10 ALMAGAMI/Shutterstock, p14 quka/Shutterstock, p16t Littlekidmoment/Shutterstock, p16b Courtesy British-Sign.co.uk, p17 S.Borisov/Shutterstock, p18tl Alex Brylov/Shutterstock, p18tr Elnur/Shutterstock, p18cl 1000 Words/Shutterstock, p18cr chrisdorney/Shutterstock, p18bl Avigator Thailand/Shutterstock, p18br Sorbis/Shutterstock, p20 Diego Schtutman/Shutterstock, p22t Claudine Klodien/Alamy Stock Photo, p22b Peter Griffin/Alamy Stock Photo, p23 Images & Stories/Alamy Stock Photo, p24t Art Directors & TRIP/Alamy Stock Photo, p24c Christian Mueller/Shutterstock, p24b Anders Blomqvist/Alamy Stock Photo, p25 Dragon Images/Shutterstock, p26 Vytautas Kielaitis/Shutterstock, p27 takayuki/Shutterstock, p28 Elnur/Shutterstock, p29 d1sk/Shutterstock, p30 Jan Miks/Alamy Stock Photo, p33t fieldwork/Shutterstock, p35 AlexLMX/Shutterstock, p36t Arkadiusz Fajer/Shutterstock, p36b T-flex/Shutterstock, p39 DVARG/Shutterstock, p40t Valentyna Chukhlyebova/Shutterstock, p40b GUDKOV ANDREY/Shutterstock, p41t GUDKOV ANDREY/Shutterstock, p41b Anna Kucherova/Shutterstock, p44t Solvin Zankl/Alamy Stock Photo, p44c Ryan Ladbrook/Shutterstock, p44b Sergey Miroshnik/Shutterstock, p45t iPortret/Shutterstock, p45bl Alexandra Lande/Shutterstock, p45br Shi Yali/Shutterstock, p47 Willyam Bradberry/Shutterstock, p48 ChameleonsEye/Shutterstock, p49 Creative Lab/Shutterstock, p51 Alexander Chaikin/Shutterstock, p52l Opas Chotiphantawanon/Shutterstock, p52tr Christopher Meder/Shutterstock, p52br Jolanda Aalbers/Shutterstock, p53 Natalia Siverina/ Shutterstock, p55l mastapiece/Shutterstock, p55r ermess/Shutterstock, p56t Larissa Kulik/Shutterstock, p56l Eugene Ivanov/Shutterstock, p56r Bruce Rolff/Shutterstock, p57l CYC/Shutterstock, p57r Eugene Ivanov/Shutterstock, p58l Papa Bravo/Shutterstock, p58cl JOAT/Shutterstock, p58cr Gigra/Shutterstock, p58r Carlos Rios (Morocco)/Alamy Stock Photo, p59 Oleg Znamenskiy/Shutterstock, p60l EvrenKalinbacak/Shutterstock, p60c Ivoha/Shutterstock, p60r Tycson1/Shutterstock, p61 Samot/Shutterstock, p62l Ammit Jack/Shutterstock, p62r EpicStockMedia/Shutterstock, p63t Mauricio Graiki/Shutterstock, p63c Dreamframer/Shutterstock, p63b Tom Grundy/Shutterstock, p65 Pikoso.kz/ Shutterstock, p66 Microgen/Shutterstock, p68l Shahril KHMD, p68r Darren Craig/Alamy Stock Photo, p71 Grant Wood/ Bridgeman Images, p73 stockphoto mania/Shutterstock, p74tl Sailorr/Shutterstock, p74tc Tupungato/Shutterstock, p74tr connel/Shutterstock, p74cl Pressmaster/Shutterstock, p74c Matej Kastelic/Shutterstock, p74cr Nick Starichenko/Shutterstock, p74b EUGENE TANNER / Stringer, p77tr petrmalinak/Shutterstock, p77tl Artisticco LLC/Alamy Stock Vector, p77cr ImageZoo/Alamy Stock Photo, p77cl monicaodo/Shutterstock, p77br Haiyin Wang/Alamy Stock Photo, p77bl Margarita Reshetnikova/Shutterstock, p79 cyo bo/Shutterstock, p80l chuyuss/Shutterstock, p80r anandoart/Shutterstock, p81 Claudio Divizia/Shutterstock, p82t Frederic Legrand – COMEO/Shutterstock, p82ct Dizfoto/Shutterstock, p82cb Galina Savina/Shutterstock, p83 Elena Schweitzer/Shutterstock, p86 LanKS/Shutterstock, p89 marekuliasz/Shutterstock, p91t SAQUIZETA/Shutterstock, p91c Tiger Images/Shutterstock, p91b pathdoc/Shutterstock, p93 Vitalii Nesterchuk/Shutterstock, p94 Artens/Shutterstock, p95 MelaniWright/Shutterstock, p96 umpo/Shutterstock, p98 WAYHOME studio/Shutterstock, p99 GUDKOV ANDREY/Shutterstock, p100l dangdumrong/Shutterstock, p100c Michael Patrick O'Neill/Alamy Stock Photo, p100r Simon Eeman/Shutterstock, p102 JonathanC Photography/Shutterstock, p103 Bildagentur Zoonar GmbH/Shutterstock, p106t Shaun Ferguson/Shutterstock, p106ct Radu Bercan/Shutterstock, p106ct fullempty/Shutterstock, p106cb SouWest Photography/Shutterstock, p106b Angel DiBilio/Shutterstock, p108l Kjersti Joergensen/Shutterstock, p108cl Gecko1968/Shutterstock, p108cr Lynnya/Shutterstock, p108r Volodymyr Burdiak/Shutterstock, p109 PSD photography/Shutterstock, p110 suwatsilp sooksang/Shutterstock, p112 Pedarilhos/Shutterstock, p114 SCOTTCHAN/Shutterstock, p115 Steve Cukrov/Shutterstock, p116 Harvepino/Shutterstock, p117 © Collins Bartholomew Ltd 2017, p120 Sergey Nivens/Shutterstock, p121 Africa Studio/Shutterstock, p122t Balinda/Shutterstock, p122b l i g h t p o e t/Shutterstock, p124l Milica Nistoran/Shutterstock, p124r Rido/Shutterstock, p125 Kitsunemedia/Shutterstock, p129 ifong/Shutterstock, p131 Kagai19927/Shutterstock, p133 Gustavo Frazao/Shutterstock, p135 4zevar/Shutterstock, p136 Alexey Y. Petrov/ Shutterstock, p141t iQoncept/Shutterstock, p142b Rawpixel.com/Shutterstock, p143 R.M. Nunes/Shutterstock, p144tl clearlens/Shutterstock, p144tr samkin/Shutterstock, p144bl LianeM/Shutterstock, p144br Tobik/Shutterstock, p146ct QUINTUS STRAUSS/Shutterstock, p146cr Sergey Uryadnikov/Shutterstock, p146br Patryk Kosmider/Shutterstock, p146t Orhan Cam/Shutterstock, p146bl © Collins Bartholomew Ltd 2017, p148l Akil Rolle-Rowan/Shutterstock, p148r irin-k/Shutterstock, p150tl Pius Lee/Shutterstock, p150tr Bildagentur Zoonar GmbH/Shutterstock, p150b World History Archive/Alamy Stock Photo, p152l Andrew Mayovskyy/Shutterstock, p152r Knot Mirai/Shutterstock, p153 Gina Smith/Shutterstock, p154 My Good Images/Shutterstock, p155t The Asahi Shimbun/Getty Images, p155c ZUMA Press, Inc./Alamy Stock Photo, p155b ZUMA Press Inc/Alamy Stock Photo, p157 Rvector/ Shutterstock, p160t Nordcry/Shutterstock, p160b Falcona/Shutterstock, p161 R.A.R. de Bruijn Holding BV/Shutterstock, p163 S-F/Shutterstock, p165 NASA, p166t 3Dsculptor/Shutterstock, p166b Andrey Armyagov/Shutterstock, p168t NASA, p168b NASA, p169t NASA, p169b NASA, p170 vicspacewalker/Shutterstock, p171b 10 FACE/Shutterstock, p172t NikoNomad/Shutterstock, p172b D1min/Shutterstock, p174 NASA, p175 Aranami/Shutterstock, p176 Algol/Shutterstock, p177 Aerofex/REX/Shutterstock, p178 studiostoks/Shutterstock, p181 Andrea Danti/Shutterstock, p186t Cheryl Casey/Shutterstock, p186ct eurobanks/Shutterstock, p186cb Julia Tsokur/Shutterstock, p186b Darren Baker/Shutterstock, p189 iurii/Shutterstock, p190 Vjom/Shutterstock